Return to Real

An Intimate Look at One Woman's Journey of Redemption

by Chalis Butler

Published by Covenant Publishing House
26 Lake Wire Drive
PO Box 524
Lakeland, Florida 33802
TheCovenantCenter.com

Book cover and interior design by Kingery Design Co.
Contributing Editor: Andi Cumbo-Floyd
Proofreader: Arnetta Jackson

Author: Chalis Butler, LoveDweller.com

Printed in the United States of America
First Printing: January 2021
Library of Congress Control Number: 2020925640
ISBN: 978-1-7360073-0-3 (Paperback)
ISBN: 978-1-7360073-1-0 (eBook)

Disclaimer: The material in this book cannot substitute for professional advice; further, the author is not liable if the reader relied on the material and was financially or otherwise damaged in some way. Also, the recollection of the stories shared are recalled to the best of the author's knowledge.

for the children

Blessed are the pure in heart, for they shall see God.
MATTHEW 5:8

CONTENTS

PREFACE

MY DESIRE IN WRITING *RETURN TO REAL* HAS BEEN TO SHARE, as thoroughly as possible, the truths and principles that led me through the healing process, an experience that essentially gave me back my life. I share my own personal story throughout, not only for the sake of transparency, but to give hope to others who might find somewhere within their own hearts a resonating with its telling.

The principles I was given and which I have written about, changed me and changed the course of my life so much for the better, that I wonder where I would be today, had I not been brought to the people and the places that served as my healing people, and my healing places—the people providing friendship, counsel and mentorship, and plenty of space to heal; the places providing the freedom to rest, to recover, to grieve, to just be and for heaven's sake—to not do.

I pray your time spent within these pages would inspire and encourage you to pursue your own heart—that you would gain new insights, discover new pathways to explore, and be given tools for deeper digging.

To all who are on a healing journey, my prayers for you are for truth in the inward parts (Psalm 51:6); for life-changing revelation of your own heart and your priceless worth; for healing that restores you to freedom and your best, most authentic self; and that you will experience the redeeming of all that's been lost along the way.

Still Returning,

Chališ

PART I

Awake

Awake, you who sleep, arise from the dead,

and Christ will give you light.

EPHESIANS 5:14

I'm Not OK

Several years ago, when my niece was about three, her favorite movie was *Madagascar*.[1] In fact, it was about the only thing she watched for a season, and we became very familiar with it. Four animals living at the zoo in New York City since birth: three of the four friends are completely unconcerned with the fact that they are being held captive, enclosed in spaces which attempt to simulate—yet are not— their habitats of origin. They are in fact, from what we can see, content with their lot and their daily routines.

Alex the Lion is happy because every day, as he emerges from his den to execute his impressive solo performance of ferocious poses as the 'King' of New York, he is praised and applauded by the crowds. His other great pleasure in life is the fresh, raw meat he is provided every day at mealtime. For these reasons, he is quite satisfied with his life at the zoo. Melman the Giraffe gets lots of attention for his aches and pains and sniffles. He is prone to all kinds of sickness (real or perceived), so he makes decisions based on all of the negative possibilities—the 'what-ifs.' He embraces

---

[1] *Madagascar*. Directed by Eric Darnell, DreamWorks Animation, 2005. Film.

his ailments as his inevitable lot in life, taking his identity from them. And Gloria, the sassy, happy-go-lucky Hippo couldn't really imagine any better place to live, as she blissfully enjoys her daily swim in her own personal pool, and sleeps to her heart's content.

And then there is Marty the Zebra. In the opening scene, we hear a glorious instrumental rendition of "Born Free" ushering us into a beautiful, wide-open paradise—lush meadows lined with tall shade trees, colorful flowers, an idyllic sky-colored lake, and vibrant green as far as the eye can see. Marty is bounding through the field, full of energy and vitality. It is clear that as he finds himself in the environment he was meant to inhabit, he is truly exhilarated. Even though he is in full motion, he is also at peace; he is completely at home, and he is relishing his total freedom. It is from this daydream that he is abruptly awakened to his reality—life at the zoo. After a dream like that, who wouldn't begin to question? *Is this all there is to life? Or is there more to it—something bigger and better? Was I really meant to live as a captive in a zoo? What if there really is something called The Wild? And if so, how do I get there?*

What about you and me? What would it look like for us to experience life as it was 'meant to be?' I imagine it would include things like:

Daily pursuit of a meaningful existence
Daily sense of gratitude, perfect peace, and authentic, deep joy
Being engaged in fulfilling, rich relationships
Freedom from inhibitions, self-criticism, fears, and judgments
Complete physical and emotional health and wholeness
Financial abundance, overflow, and freedom
No limits, no ceilings, no cages
Unlimited opportunity to pursue dreams and desires

As I write this, I am sitting at Panera. I come to the same Panera every Wednesday morning as early as I can get myself out of the house. I order the same thing, I sit at the same table, and I stare out the window at the same Swan Hotel across the street, every Wednesday morning. I'm usually one of the first customers to arrive, but after about an hour, the tables around me begin to fill up, and the conversations that surround my table make it hard for me to think. Eventually, I pull out my headphones and I crank up my rain storm app to drown out the voices.

This morning, I decided to search Pandora for some music. I searched for "relaxing music." What surged through my headphones and into my slightly irritated senses was something that so moved me that it invited me to pause: I close my eyes...I take a deep breath... and I accept the invitation—to listen, to soak in the beauty of it, to get lost in it, and to put all of my worries on hold—just for this moment.

The song that is playing is an instrumental piece that is rich and vibrant, even in its simplicity; it is passionate and exhilarating. At the same time, it is completely peaceful, relaxing, and soothing. It is also inspiring, redemptive, hopeful ... how can one song be all of these things? But this song is all of this—more even—and it utterly captures me.

Afterwards, as I think about what it represents to me, tears come to my eyes. *This is not what we experience most of the time. This is not how life feels for most of us. But it is what we long for! Vibrancy, passion, a hopeful excitement about life. Freedom from fears, worries, and stress; rest, beauty, and peace.*

Isn't there a longing in all of us to experience life as it was meant to be? Is it possible to attain this kind of life? We are searching for it, each in our own way. Many of us can attest to having looked in all the wrong places—but we are looking for it. We long for the fulfillment of these desires that are nestled somewhere deep within us.

Notice that nearly all of the things we long for are qualities of an inner state of being—they are not outward or material desires.

.at we hope to experience *on the inside*. Even that which
be an outward or material desire, such as financial
e, represents something immaterial. An abundance of
or most represents freedom. This may be time freedom,
or freedom to meet personal needs or desires easily, or it may just
represent security and freedom from fear of the unexpected.

Although our longings are for things not visible from the outside, in our attempt to create our best life, we are often driven to
pursue the outward things. For example, we may spend all of our
time and energy pursuing what we believe to be worthy interests
such as healthy eating and exercise, practicing meditation, using
positive language, self-improvement through self-help books and
online courses, being involved with social justice organizations,
giving to charities, church attendance and service, goal setting,
entrepreneurial endeavors, networking and making connections,
keeping an active social life, building and establishing a respectable
career, acquiring material wealth, and more.

Some of us, like Alex The Lion, find ourselves performing for
the applause of men. This could come from an outwardly 'put together' appearance as a successful business man/woman, or as a
homeschooling mom who can make it look easy, or as the person
everyone can count on to get the job done at work or at church. There
is nothing intrinsically wrong with being efficient, successful, or
admirable. But sometimes, even though we enjoy receiving admiration and praise from others, on the *inside* there can be something
that feels like a 'disconnect' or like something is missing. It can start
to feel tiring or even seem impossible to try and hold it all together
any longer. There may even be a feeling of loneliness or feeling far
away from people or God because somehow, it is difficult to really
get close to anyone.

The character of Melman the Giraffe epitomizes a mindset that
many of us unknowingly return to again and again: we are victims.

We are underdogs. We are helpless against our circumstances. Others should have sympathy, and should understand that this is just the way things are for us. Whether it is literally ongoing physical ailments, perceived rejection from others, or feeling hurt, disregarded, overlooked, or offended on a regular basis. This can be a comfort zone. What might be underneath this? After all, it is not rational to 'enjoy' sickness, rejection, or helplessness. How could this be a comfort zone for anyone?

And then, there's Gloria the Hippo—content with the simple pleasures of life, not really focused on what is missing, but instead, looking on the bright side and filling up her time and days with things that feel good. This kind of life can seem to satisfy for a long time, but there can come a time when it is just not enough anymore. We wake up one day and wonder *Is this all there is to it? Is feeling good or being happy (because I've got life's comforts to keep me entertained/comfortable/occupied/numb) really what we were created for? Is this really what I want my life to be about?*

As diligently as we may work to build our best life through outward pursuits, there remains an incongruence that keeps us from genuinely experiencing life as it was meant to be. For every outward appearance, there is an inward reality that, for many, does not align with what is visible from the outside. In fact, there can be a chasm that lies between our inward and outward realities. And this can be true whether or not we are aware of it. In fact, many times we are completely unaware of this dynamic at all, not only because we are deeply entrenched in our familiar way of doing life and the well-worn paths and patterns of our thought processes, but because we have learned so well how to bury many of our inward emotions in order to maintain that outward reality, to the point that we have become quite numb to our emotions. We are focused on all of the outward things—while the inner life is pushed aside again and again. And so, the incongruence between what others (and even we ourselves) can see from the outside and what lies within us goes unnoticed and unaddressed.

Most of us are doing our best to make life work for us, when at some point, for one reason or another, something disrupts our status quo. Maybe life begins to feel monotonous, boring, or even meaningless. Maybe too much disappointment has left me broken, and I just feel done. Maybe things start to feel completely out of control. Maybe I am blindsided by some major loss or event. Maybe the pressure of holding things together day in and day out begins to feel too heavy, until finally, I feel like 'I just can't do this anymore!' Or maybe several things happen all at once to create the perfect storm, and as a result, my world begins to feel like it is falling apart. Whatever it looks like, there comes a point for most of us when we just feel like *something needs to change*.

If you can identify (a little or a lot) with what I have described, then you may be more of a Marty the Zebra than you know. Marty woke up on the morning of his birthday from a dream that painted another picture—a much higher picture—than what he was currently experiencing, and on that day, he began to feel *not OK* with his current reality. He began questioning it out loud and challenging his friends about it too. He began wondering if there was a way to get to The Wild. Not only did his friends not understand his discontentment, they did not like it at all. They discouraged him from even the thought of venturing out. They said it would not be safe, that it would be silly and dangerous because there probably was no Wild anyway. They liked life the way it was. But something in Marty *knew there was more*.

Many of us, if we are honest, can identify with more than one of these characters, their mindsets, and their habits. I have had a little of all of them in me. A crossroads moment in my early thirties, when I felt like I had failed at everything that mattered, was the low point I needed to get to, in order to wake up to my reality—I was living a much smaller life than I was meant to live. I was Alex the Lion—performing to gain the approval of others. I was Melman the Giraffe—victim to my circumstances, ever fending off depression. I was Gloria the Hippo—nestling up to my creature comforts, blind to my captivity. But just like Marty the Zebra, thankfully, I came to a place where the way I had always functioned *just wasn't working for me anymore.*

The bottom line was, I was not OK. And I hadn't really been OK for a long time, but I was coping with life in all of the learned ways I had collected that had allowed me to get by, and at times, even made me feel like I was doing pretty well. It sounds strange to say it, but until that crossroads moment happened for me, I was truly unaware of how 'not OK' I really was.

THE GREAT LOSS

Crossroads moments are so incredibly important. They are especially significant because it almost always takes a crossroads moment to open our eyes to our own part of what I will call The Great Loss.

The Great Loss is the loss we have all faced, to some degree or another, of the full, rich, beautiful life we were meant to live. It can mean the loss of a loving, secure home and family in which to have experienced my childhood, as every child deserves; it can mean the loss of courage to face life, loss of self-love, loss of freedom to dream and succeed; it can mean years or decades that were stolen because I spent them being anything and everything but my true self; it can mean a life-long pattern of sabotaging the deep, meaningful relationships that we all long for. It looks different for everyone, but because we live in an imperfect world, with imperfect parents and teachers and friends and situations—all imperfect—we have all experienced The Great Loss to some extent. And for many, it has brought us to a place of living one way on the outside, while on the inside, if we are honest with ourselves, we are not OK.

It is a great mercy to come to a crossroads moment and realize that we are coming to the end of ourselves, that there must be more, and that we are becoming truly desperate for something to change.

There is hope, and there is light ahead. There is a way that leads to the kind of life that isn't just about existing or surviving; it isn't about keeping the plates spinning, and it isn't even about keeping ourselves comfortable. It's a different kind of life than so many are experiencing. For me, the feeling I noticed once I began to experience this different kind of life, was that I felt like I had just begun to *really live*. No more trying to hold things together (or trying to appear to have it all together), no more trying to get on top of my life in all of its little compartments, making sure each one was in perfect working order; no more trying to force my own pictures of what my life was 'supposed' to look like into the severely limited frames of my present reality (and failing repeatedly); no more sinking slowly into cycles of shame, depression, isolation, and self-medication. No more.

There is a way that leads to LIFE. "Behold, You desire truth in the inward parts, and in the hidden part, You will make me to know wisdom," (Psalm 51:6). This became my prayer—"God, show me the truth in the inward parts. What is really going on inside of me?" And He answered this prayer. My life was literally changed in a remarkable way. And this gift, this new way, is available for whosoever will.

QUESTIONS TO CONSIDER

If you had to choose one of the characters of Madagascar with whom you identify the most, would it be Alex the Lion, Melman the Giraffe, Gloria the Hippo, or Marty the Zebra? Write about why.

Take some time to consider how you might imagine life as it was meant to be. Make your own written list of what this might look like. Do you feel like you are currently experiencing this kind of life?

How is life working for you? Have you experienced anything in the last few months or years that causes you to feel like things are being shaken up?

Then Jacob was left alone; and a Man wrestled with

him until the breaking of day. Now when He saw

that He did not prevail against him, He touched the

socket of his hip; and the socket of Jacob's hip was

out of joint as He wrestled with him. And He said,

"Let Me go, for the day breaks." But he said,

"I will not let You go unless You bless me!"

GENESIS 32: 24-26

CHAPTER 2

Rewired

SO WHAT EXACTLY IS THIS NEW AND DIFFERENT WAY ALL
about? Well, I'll tell you what it's *not* about. It is not about resolving
to change my behaviors. How long does a New Year's resolution
typically last, for example? How hard is it for most of us to break an
old habit and start a new one? At the very least, we could probably
agree that it doesn't come naturally; and that, in fact, it takes an
incredible amount of willpower and personal determination to create a new habit. Simply 'deciding' to make a change does not come
easily because a new behavior or habit does not flow naturally out
of what is really inside of us.

For true change in a life, something on the inside must be
rewired. Why rewired? Because we are living and functioning out
of deeply held, false beliefs. There are beliefs we hold to that are
so deeply ingrained within us, that they have become a part of
our identity and our life paradigm. These are our Heart Beliefs. It
is as though we are *wired* to respond to people and circumstances
a certain way because of these Heart Beliefs. There is no easy way
to change this, particularly when we are not even aware of what

we truly believe at our core. We are, in a way, at the mercy of these Heart Beliefs. The interesting thing is that even if we try to act in opposition to them, the Heart Beliefs (what is really inside of us) will still find their way out, even when we are working to mask them or trying to keep them pushed down. Trying to live in opposition to how we are wired is exhausting, and can't be kept up forever.

The truth is, we are *compelled* to do what we do because it is how we are wired. We are often compelled to do things we don't even want to do—because these Heart Beliefs are 'in charge,' so to speak.

This might be OK if everything we believe deep down were always true. The problem is that many of our deeply held Heart Beliefs are simply not based in truth. They are lies. And these false Heart Beliefs determine our actions, much more so than what we have learned and know with our minds and speak with our mouths.

For the sake of this discussion, I will use the term "Mind Belief" to refer to all that we know and believe intellectually--with the mind. A simple example of the incongruence that lies between a Heart Belief and a Mind Belief would be when we say something like, "God is good" (because we have been taught this and believe it with our mind) when really, we don't deeply believe God is good, because if we did, we would be at complete peace about many things that in reality, cause us anxiety, pain, or anger. Another example could be an emotion we harbor, unaware. "I trust God with everything in my life." Deep down, I might harbor bitterness and distrust toward God, not believing at all that God is going to come through for me, because after all, Where was He when I was being abused? When I lost my mom? When my father left? When tragedy struck our home? He did not come through for me then, so why should I trust Him now?

And what follows? Rather than living in a way that reflects the notion that God is good and that He is trustworthy, we may try to control our circumstances, anticipating every possible thing that could go wrong, making decisions out of fear and worry because we don't actually believe God is good and we don't trust Him. Or, maybe we deaden our longings and push down our dreams because we fear the disappointment we will experience if God doesn't come through in the way that we think He should.

Another Heart Belief might be about Self, such as a deeply held notion that I am 'rejectable.' Here's how that false Heart Belief can work in me, compelling me to sabotage my relationships: I believe deep down that I am 'rejectable'—that others should, and will, reject me. Because I believe this about myself, I will actually *invite others to reject me* through my actions, words, and body language. And guess what? They will often comply with my belief and accept my invitation. So at times, I will experience real rejection from others, and other times, it may just be a perceived rejection because I have already assumed I will be rejected. Therefore, I may perceive/receive someone's actions as rejection, even when they are not intending to reject me. Either way, over and over, I will experience the pain of rejection, and end up feeling lonely and sorry for myself. If I am living with a Heart Belief that I am unacceptable or 'rejectable,' then I will continually experience this dynamic—until something changes.

Now, I can become aware of this, but I cannot change my Heart Beliefs simply by telling myself something different. I am already telling myself something different every day, and knowing and believing it with my mind. The Heart Beliefs are not formed with words and information—they are formed by what we have experienced, especially in our early years, but also throughout our life. For a Heart Belief to change, there must be a rewiring.

SYDNEY

Through my twenties, I was searching—for meaning, for answers, for relief from my own reality. My story was not unfolding the way I'd imagined it should, so I was always up for adventure, because for me, an adventure meant hope that whatever I was searching for could be just around the corner.

A few years after graduating college, I was sitting with some friends one day, and one of them started talking about a church in Australia that we were all familiar with. He was talking about their music, and that they had a leadership school, and that he was thinking he might go to Sydney, and would I like to come too?

Would I like to come too? *Um, Yes, please!* I was ecstatic at the thought of doing something different, and intrigued with what it would be like to experience life in another part of the world. So I went for it. I renewed my passport, moved home, paid off debt, saved money, sold my car, and bought my ticket.

I arrived in Sydney in May of 2005. I was a student again at 28, and the adventure of this intriguing new world was just what the doctor ordered. I was enraptured with Sydney's beaches: gorgeous massive rock cliffs and the biggest, crashiest, waves I'd ever seen. I soaked up the novelty of city living. I rode buses, taxis, and trains, and I walked a lot. I discovered Aussie ('Ozzie,' not 'Ossie') coffee, and how yummy croissants can be when you stuff them with strips of hard chocolate. I learned the word 'patisserie.' I learned to say 'cutlery' instead of 'silverware,' and 'that's pretty cool, *hey.*' Instead of 'that's pretty cool, huh?' and to order food 'take away' instead of 'to go.' I learned about brekky and bickies and dummies, and I learned that fries are chips and chips are crisps. 'No worries' and 'lovely' and 'heaps' became a part of my personal vernacular. I also learned there was such a thing as butternut squash soup. Who knew? I found out what it means to 'take the mickey out of' someone, and I ate my very-first-ever, honest-to-goodness crumpet. With Vegemite.

But even more valuable than this veritable fortune of Australian jargon I picked up, was the opportunity I had to meet, and fall in love with, people from all over the world. I met people from England,

Canada, Israel, France, Switzerland, Germany, Italy, India, Russia, Czech Republic, South Korea, Finland, Norway, Sweden, Brazil, Nigeria, South Africa, and of course Australia. And the people I met were salt-of-the-earth people. They were unassuming, and so beautiful. Experiencing another country and its culture and, essentially, so much more of the world through all of these beautiful people, were the gifts of this adventure.

The third year I was in Australia, I started working with a small church about an hour north of Sydney, leading music and helping with the youth group. While the experience of the leadership school had been exciting—never a dull moment—the transition to this small, personal place began to reveal and hone in on some of my deeper desires for depth in relationship and connection. I was loving this place. My job description, aside from leading music on Sundays and helping with the youth, was to spend time in prayer, vision sessions, writing music, and studying—all things I loved. And I was being mentored and led by someone I had great respect for and who believed there was something worth championing in me.

In time, we began to ask questions that eventually led us to the decision to close down our traditional Sunday morning services and morph ourselves into a house church. There was so much mixture in this process for me. Our desire for deeper, stronger relationships and a more genuine expression of God's love was sincere. But in truth, what we were trying to build through the vision we were bringing to this group of people, was a utopian community. We were all longing for something more—more honest conversations and more meaningful connection. These are all valid longings, yet creating a utopian community requires, subtly or otherwise, some measure of control. We try to control because somewhere along the way, we lost the freedom to trust. We *must* get our own needs met—whatever that takes; we *must* self-protect—because we have been so badly hurt before; we *must* create a safe world—because feeling out of control is terrifying. This is not freedom, and this is not how we were meant to live. A utopian community cannot exist here because there are no utopian, a.k.a. perfect, people. And so, looking back now, I believe that the motives behind our efforts were both pure and impure, because they rested within the unhealed, wounded hearts of people whose love for God could not nullify the brokenness within their souls.

We are whole persons with deeply ingrained Heart Beliefs that compel us into our behaviors, and when we are living with unhealed wounds from the past, the worthy, God-given, noble desires are intermingled with the unmet longings, deficiencies, and voids we are trying to fill. Without our consent, and often without our awareness, one pulls stronger and calls louder to us than the other. The voids, the deficiencies *feel the truest,* so they become the more compelling of the two. Our vision can begin to be *driven* by our unmet longings and voids, rather than being *led* by the Holy Spirit. Perhaps this is why God often allows our seemingly worthy pursuits to fail. Perhaps succeeding in these pursuits would cause more damage than good, to others and ourselves. Perhaps we are constantly experiencing His mercy, and only every now and then, recognizing it.

In the midst of all of this, I was witnessing, and very much accomplice to, the tearing down of all I had known of the most long-standing, consistent, and foundational practice of my faith—going to church. For a lifetime, I had been taught that this is what it means to 'forsake not the assembling of yourselves.' I remember at three years old, sitting on the front row of our little church while my dad preached, knowing that if we made too much noise, my mom would take us out the front door (directly behind the pulpit) and spank us, and that if that happened, we'd get another one from my dad when we got home. We were quiet little mice. I also remember standing on a chair next to my dad behind the same wide, wooden pulpit, singing "Gentle Shepherd" with him, while my mom accompanied us on piano. For as long as I could remember, church was not optional, it was a requirement. You can't just *not* go to church.

The deconstructing, the 'what ifs,' and the progressive discussions were a wrecking ball to the dwelling place of my beliefs, my upbringing, and my experience of the church and Christianity. Every question led to another question. And even though I believe there was value in the questions we were asking, for me, this course led me to a much greater disillusionment, because although I was genuinely searching for truth and meaning, underneath it all, I was broken, and angry. The spirituality that I had always turned to as an answer to my pain was now suspect, and with good reason. It's not that the Scriptures were untrue. They were true—they will always be true. I just held opposing (false) beliefs at my core (my heart) that felt much truer than the Scriptures I believed with my mind. And the disconnect between my head and my heart meant that at some point, I would either have to reconcile them, or choose between the two once and for all.

We cannot *will* our wounds to stop affecting us. We cannot quote any amount of Scripture that will rid us of them. God has created within us a natural grief process by which we are able to experience His healing. Without grieving our losses, without healing, we remain wounded. And wounds must be healed, not cast out or overcome.

One reason I believe this is such a vital distinction to make is that when we ignore or try to blot out the past, we are essentially throwing away an integral part of our story. We don't just learn from our mistakes, although we do that too. We are destined—we are actually being called—to learn and grow and become bigger and deeper, and stronger and more compassionate, and truly more lovely, having more to offer the world—much, much more than we otherwise would have—*because of what we have been through.* Oswald Chambers calls it being 'broken bread and poured out wine.'[1]

---

1   *Oswald Chambers,* The Love of God (Grand Rapids, MI: Oswald Chambers Publication Association, 1988).

Yes, there is a sense of having 'overcome' trauma or tragedy, simply by virtue of surviving it. Yet if, in time, that event or that wound still holds power over us; if it stops us from being fully alive, from living and loving without fear, from embracing and practicing vulnerability; if it keeps us stuck or struggling with addictions; if it limits us or makes us believe ourselves to be smaller than we really are, then have we really overcome it? Or has it overcome us?

I have been quoted Scriptures about forgetting the past (Philippians 3:13,14). Paul is not telling us to just erase all of our memories. He is talking about forgetting our own failures and past sins so that we can "press toward the goal for the prize of the upward call of God in Christ Jesus." Choosing to look at the past has been one of the most challenging things I've done. It has been *only* through a purposeful pursuit of healing—fighting for my own heart—that I have been able to grow in courage and freedom to move forward, pressing into this upward call.

Paul, who wrote Philippians, was a 'Hebrew of Hebrews,' and in the Hebrew culture, remembrance of the past is a deeply and dearly held value. God often told men to build memorials because He wanted them to *remember* what they had been through, and His faithfulness in the midst of it. Skip Moen writes about remembering in one of his daily word studies:

> *In Hebraic thought, it is the future that is behind us. That's why we can't see it. It is behind our heads, out of the capacity of our eyes, and therefore unknown. We see the past. That's what is in front of us. We can look into the past to see what God has already done. We remember His faithfulness because it is already visible to us. We are men and women, rowing in a boat, always looking where we have been, but never actually seeing where we are going.*[2]

---
[2]   *Moen, Skip.* "Face Forward." Skip Moen, April 2014. https://skipmoen.com/2014/04/face-forward/.

To move forward, we face backward. We acknowledge where we have been. Yet, to do this honestly, we have to reconcile all the things we see when we look back; reconcile what we say we believe with what our hearts may feel as we remember painful things. *If God is faithful, where was He when that happened? If God is good, why didn't He protect me? How can I trust God when I feel like He has betrayed me?*

These are the hard questions. They are hard, but more importantly they are real, and they are honest, and they address the disconnect between what we have been taught and 'know,' and what we really believe, deep down. And unless we are willing to wrestle with these questions like Jacob wrestled with God, our lives *will* reflect the incongruence residing within us, despite all of our most ardent efforts to the contrary.

This is an important part of the Rewiring—asking hard questions. If there are behaviors and habits we struggle to overcome, identifying and acknowledging false Heart Beliefs, as well as the incongruence between those Heart Beliefs and our Mind Beliefs, is a necessary, foundational part of the process. Being willing to 'go there' and ask the hard questions has been a vital part of allowing myself to be "rewired," and it has been a beautiful journey of discovery that has led me, really and truly, to a new and different way of living.

QUESTIONS TO CONSIDER

Have you ever found yourself responding to situations or circumstances in ways that you don't want to respond?

Take some time to consider whether or not there might be any incongruence between your Heart Beliefs and Mind Beliefs.

Often, people like to use the expression "just let it go" referring to pain from the past. Yet, hurts that continue to resurface even after years or decades have passed, may still need to be grieved. Can you think of a situation from the past that you have tried to "let go" of, but that you maybe have not given yourself permission to face, process, or grieve?

You have no idea how safe you really are.

JESS RAY

"DIMENSIONS" FROM THE ALBUM
SENTIMENTAL CREATURES

CHAPTER 3

Ready or Not?

IN 2010, TWO YEARS AFTER RETURNING FROM SYDNEY, MY life fell completely apart. I will share more specifically about it, but essentially it was this 'falling apart' that awakened me to acknowledge and experience my emotions honestly for the first time, without having to make sure my belief system remained intact at all costs.

This brought me to a place where I was desperate for the truth, no matter the cost. I had come to such a low point in my life, that I no longer had any illusions that I could ever hope to get things right without knowing the whole truth—whatever that looked like.

Among other things, getting down to the truth involves making a decision to be willing to let go of everything we cling to in our efforts to keep it together. Is this easy? Yes and No. The easy part—the part that is a tremendous relief—is the part where I stop trying to maintain the appearance of having it all together. (Who was buying it anyway?) It is a relief to stop trying to please everyone. It is a relief when the weight of the world is lifted off because for the first time, I don't feel responsible for how everyone else feels. It is a relief not to feel like I have to smile politely when inside I just want to burst into tears, or blurt out something really honest. It is a relief to be able to say to myself—*Self, you are a mess, and that's OK.*

But the hard part is substantial. There is, of course, the past. This thought in itself can be overwhelming. There are hurts and fears to be faced. I will disappoint people. There are dynamics in my relationships that will be severely disrupted. There will be change. I will be vulnerable and I will feel exposed. I will become raw. I will experience emotions I have successfully avoided for years. There will be pain and possibly humiliation. There will probably be a lot of tears.

So . . . who's ready to sign up?

This brings to mind an experience I had several years ago. I have always hated going to the doctor and I always put it off as long as I can. But desperation can cause us to do things we don't really want to do, things we wouldn't ordinarily do. We can 'maintain' for a long time without actually being healthy or thriving. Well, at one point, several health-related issues began cropping up. Combined, they began to grab my attention, so much so, that finally I became desperate and made a doctor's appointment.

After meeting with the doctor, he prescribed me daily vitamin B shots. Before I could leave, the nurse had to talk me through the process of giving myself a shot in the leg. Somehow, to my surprise, I was able to execute this successfully. I gathered my supplies and headed back out to the waiting room. My thoughts wandered . . . *Well, I think that went pretty well, considering I literally just stabbed myself in the leg. On purpose.* As I was considering this, I was nearing the front desk when the room began to move and sway and flash around me. *Whoooa.* I quickly located the nearest chair. The nurse came back for me, and as we were walking back to the exam room, she nonchalantly said over her shoulder, "Yeah, sometimes it happens. The mind doesn't know what to think because, y' know, it's not really natural to inflict pain on your own body."

Indeed. It is most certainly *not* natural to inflict pain on your own body—yet in a way, this is what it is to choose to pursue healing. For by choosing this we are saying, *Yes, God, I give you permission to take me into the painful memories—to the moments marked by shame, betrayal, sadness, abandonment, devastation. Help me not only to remember them, but walk with me as I experience the emotions surrounding them. Take me into the pain; bring on the tears. Show me every injustice, every loss, and make a way for me to fully grieve all that was lost.*

Everything good comes at a price. Thriving in my business; enjoying a healthy marriage; raising happy, respectful kids; experiencing optimal health, as well as physical strength and fitness; excelling as an athlete, a musician, an artist, a writer, a doctor. All require tremendous sacrifice, perseverance, and a daily purposeful pursuit. Pressing in, we embrace the mixture of pain and pleasure because to us, it is worth it. Whatever 'it' is—we don't want to do life without it.

And so it goes with our mental and emotional well-being. What is it worth?

We are all in different places on our journey, and every journey is unique. Timing is important. Maybe you are content and fulfilled in your life, and maybe you don't relate to what you have read. For some, now might not be the right time. For others, what I have shared resonates.

Wherever you are on this spectrum, I encourage you to spend some time asking your questions. Maybe you have questions to ask yourself. Maybe you want some answers from God. So ask your questions. Ask, wait, and listen. We all do this differently too. Take a quiet walk by the lake. Cozy down in a comfy chair with pen, journal and a hot cup of tea. Take a long drive in the country. Play an instrument. Go fishing or hiking. Make a date with your laptop and a latte at your favorite coffee shop.

QUESTIONS TO CONSIDER

As you have read the first chapters of this book, how has it made you feel?

Would you say that doing life 'your way' is working for you? (Are you getting the results in life you want?)

Being honest with yourself, do you feel deep down that you are truly 'OK' or 'not OK?' Ask yourself: Am I content and at peace with my present lot in life? What do I long for? Do I feel 'stuck' in one or more areas of my life?

PART II

Keys

Little girls, like butterflies, need no excuse.

ROBERT HEINLEIN

AMERICAN SCIENCE-FICTION AUTHOR

CHAPTER 4

Meeting My Own Heart

BY THE TIME I GOT TO THE PLACE WHERE I WAS READY TO pursue deep healing, I had been to several counselors throughout my twenties and thirties. I searched continually for some kind of clarity about myself and the answer to this question that would come up every few years: "Where do I go from here?" In truth, I was looking for better ways to cope with how my life *wasn't* turning out, and I often found the help that I sought. I found that many counselors like to work on behavior modification, goal setting, changing thought patterns, etc. This is not bad, but it can miss the roots and the whys behind our thoughts and behaviors.

Unfortunately, finding new ways to cope with my dissatisfaction with life only prolonged the inevitable—time and again, I would dream of new roads and directions to take and I would start out in strong pursuit. But each time the newness of things would wear off, my inner reality remained. I struggled for too many years with depression. I also lived with discontentment, self-doubt, shame, insecurity, and loneliness. There was an abiding sadness that colored my in-between times, relenting only as my time was being filled with social pursuits, entertainment, relationships (always failing), and daydreams of the future.

Setting goals, dreaming new dreams, and modifying thoughts and behaviors was not enough to make any lasting change. But then one day, I had come to the end of myself. God knew that I had come to a place of desperation and true surrender. This is when He led me to someone who held KEYS. These KEYS were what made things click for me. They unlocked doors for me, enabling me to understand the truth about myself and the big picture of my life. They made it possible for me to get to the roots of what was causing so many recurring issues in my life.

It was as though I had been lost, wandering in circles in a dark forest, searching in vain for a way out, with a constant, thick fog limiting my vision and my sense of direction. As my counselor began to share these KEYS with me, the fog was lifting, and the dark, confusing forest was becoming a bright, peaceful woodland with a clear pathway underneath my feet leading to the expectant, outside world that awaited.

SHE CHANGES EVERYTHING

When I first began my healing journey, I started writing a blog to solidify what I was experiencing for myself, and to share what I was learning with others. It was the first time I had ever even considered 'putting myself out there.' Here is the first blog article I wrote and published:

> Seeing a picture of a girl you've never met, and meeting a little girl and spending time with her, are two very different experiences. Shuffling through my childhood pictures, I was looking at pictures of a girl I didn't know. Unemotional about her, I found it interesting to think back about things that happened and to talk about how they might have influenced the way that

I operate now as an adult—how I think, how I see myself, how I interact with people, etc.

But now it was time to meet her. Timing was perfect because just the year before, I had welcomed my niece into the world, and had immediately fallen madly in love. She was a delight just because she existed and boy, was I ever the doting aunt! When I set out to meet the little girl that was me, all I had to do was to picture my precious niece and my eyes would fill up with tears— this was the little girl in the pictures—an innocent, vulnerable little girl, big eyes, full of questions. This was me! How did I feel about her? How did it make me feel to see her smile? To see her laughing? To see tears streaming down her face?

When I finally truly met this sweet girl, I wanted more than anything else to find out who she was. I wanted to really know her. I was on a mission. And you know what? The more I got to know her, the more I began to discover how great she was—how beautiful she really was.

"Your eyes saw my substance, being yet unformed," (Psalm 139:16). Somewhere in the beginning, I lost sight of her. Yet God has always had her in His sight. All the years I have rejected my own heart, He has not. Where I have judged her and called her unacceptable, He has called her acceptable. Where I have hated and shamed her for being needy and messy, He has loved her *just for being*. And what else are children if not needy and messy? How much *freedom* came just from getting this one thing: she (my heart) is needy, *and that's OK*. She is messy, and that's OK. After a lifetime of being *not OK*, this revelation was such a gift to me!

From the moment I began to give my heart a voice, I knew that something was happening. Out of my darkest hour had come a desperate cry to God—*Lord, help!! Something has to change!* And when I truly connected with her for the first time (this little girl in the pictures), I knew that somehow, she was a key to this change—whatever it would be. She is who God originally made me to be—who I was Before.

She was delightful. She was vulnerable. She was uninhibited. She trusted. She was easy to love. She still is. She is lovely. She is sweet. She is honest. She loves people. She is OK just being herself. She is fearless. She is wise, and strong, and good.

And *she changes everything.*

THE HEART

What is the Heart? Although there are many definitions and uses of this word, one way Webster defines 'Heart' is this: "(a) the central or innermost part: center (b) the essential or most vital part of something."

Central. Innermost. Center. Essential. Vital.

My heart then, is who I am at the center of my being—at my core. My heart is the essential or most vital part of me. The word 'vital' implies that the heart is a necessary part in order to have life. Just as a vital organ must be functioning properly in order for physical life to be sustained, the heart (the central, innermost part) must be awake and thriving in order to have life. We might say then, that the heart must be awake and thriving in order for us to be *really living* versus *merely existing.*

How do I know if my heart is awake and thriving? This is tricky. We are so used to this word 'heart' that we can easily think we know what it means. It is a warm and fuzzy word. It is familiar and lovely, and it is spiritual and I always felt a draw to it, but I would also kind of breeze over it, never stopping too long to try to figure it out. One of the most important KEYS I was handed when I first began with my counselor was a way to understand my own heart that was tangible and simple. Well, kind of simple. Here it is:

KEY NUMBER 1
MY HEART = MYSELF, AS A LITTLE GIRL

The little girl that was me, is who I am at my core, and she exists in the present, not just the past. Seeing her with open and accepting, compassionate eyes is KEY to discovering the truth about who I am, what I have really believed (my Heart Beliefs), my emotions (the ones I feel and recognize, as well as some that I don't), and my true needs and desires.

Who was this little girl? What did she feel? What did she think? What did she love and treasure? What made her smile and laugh? If I can figure out the answers to these questions, and keep asking these kinds of questions, I can begin to know my own heart.

To discover my own heart for the first time, I had to get away from the abstract, overused, hard-to-put-my-finger-on word, 'heart.' It opened a new world of revelation to me to be able to see my heart as something (some*one*) other than the person that I looked at in the mirror every morning. Because for some reason, most of us don't have any trouble directing our contempt, criticism, shame, and anger at the woman or the man in the mirror. But to think about it from a different perspective—to realize that I am treating a little girl or a little boy this way—this is different.

Someone can counsel me to love myself, speak kindly, and be good to myself. But firstly, this is behavior modification and does not address the root of the issue or the Heart Beliefs, and secondly, we cannot truly love what we do not know, see, or understand. And I did not know my own heart. I did not understand the buried emotions or the false beliefs that resided within me, or why I felt like I just couldn't get close to people, or why God felt so far away. I didn't know what I longed for, what I wanted or needed, or where the line should be between meeting the needs of others and taking care of myself.

So the heart within me—who I am at my core—is the little girl in my childhood photos. This little girl has been with me all this time.

QUESTIONS TO CONSIDER

When you look at the man or the woman in the mirror, how do you feel about him/her?

Close your eyes and picture yourself as a child. How do you feel about that little boy or little girl?

Take some time to remember and write down several childhood memories. They can be about anything—happy or sad memories, a story, a memory of a like or dislike, a favorite toy, doll, or blanket.

We must never forget any part of ourselves. As of this writing, I am sixty-one years old in chronology. But I am not an isolated, chronological numerical statistic. I am sixty-one, and I am also four, and twelve, and fifteen, and twenty-three, and thirty-one and forty-five, and... and... and... If we lose any part of ourselves, we are thereby diminished. If I cannot be thirteen and sixty-one simultaneously, part of me has been taken away.

MADELEINE L'ENGLE

WALKING ON WATER

CHAPTER 5

Childhood

FOR ME, REMEMBERING MY CHILDHOOD BRINGS UP A mixture—lots of happy memories, and some hard memories mixed in. I want to paint a picture of how things were for me growing up, because it will be important to have some context as I share more of my healing story.

The first house I remember living in was a two-story, white house with black trim. Our house was situated a backyard or so away from the main highway that coasted straight through our tiny town in rural Wyoming. Baggs, Wyoming, is not much bigger than the dot that marks it on the map, but it was home, and it remains indelibly etched on my heart, slightly rose-colored, as the wonderful world of all of my favorite memories. Probably because it was here, in this tiny northwestern town, where all was well with my world.

One vivid memory I have of my childhood here is the cattle drive. From time to time, a herd of cattle could be heard making its way toward us from Somewhere. The highway being its footpath, the herd would pretty soon approach the stretch of road that ran past our house, prodding and jostling each other forward (or mostly forward) on their way to Somewhere Else. We would be playing in the yard and hear them coming, and we'd run up to the fence to watch the cows and the cowboys high up on their horses, rounding up and redirecting the renegades. It was captivating. Sometimes it was cows, and sometimes it was sheep. But it was always dusty and always noisy, and always worth taking a break from the business of our play, to watch.

One year, we raised four sheep in our backyard. We got them as lambs, and what I remember most about this was watching my mom prepare their bottles, being anxious to help feed them, and while I waited, the distinct, milky smell of the formula. We fed them from nipple-capped coke bottles.

We also raised chickens. I can remember coming home from school and heading straight for the tool shed where my dad had situated the fish tank, abuzz with fuzzy chicks. I would crouch down on the floor to watch them, and I can still hear their tiny *peep-peep-peeps* as they bumped around the tank, keeping warm together with the help of a heat lamp. They were probably looking for their mama. They grew up into chickens, of course, and I remember catching and feeding them grasshoppers through the chicken-wire fence. I'm sitting here wondering, *When, and why, do we lose the guts to catch grasshoppers?* I could hold frogs and lizards and grasshoppers as a kid, but now? Forget it. I *cannot* do it.

Besides sheep and chickens, we also had rabbits and dogs and horny toads. No cats though, because my dad didn't like cats. But what I really always wanted as a little girl—what I dreamed of and begged for and wished upon stars for—was a horse.

Oh, how I wanted a horse of my own! When a neighbor came around on her horse and invited me to climb up into the saddle with her, this little girl's heart was *simply elated*. I can still feel the excitement, my heart *beaming* that I was getting to ride on a *real* horse! I could never have imagined then, how encounters later in life would obliterate my courage and faith in the goodness of horses. Now, alongside this sweet memory I have of adoring all-things-horses, some less-sweet memories come to mind: severe allergies manifesting when I rode horses with some family friends in my teens; riding half-wild horses in Haiti and subsequently reconsidering my preference for horses; ranch-sitting for a family in Australia and discovering that actually, *horses are terrifying.*

I'm chuckling at myself, but there is also sadness for me in sharing this because as I reflect on it, I am recognizing the robbery in this disillusionment. As a little girl, there was a purity in the affinity for—and faith in—something that in reality, was beautiful and good. Over time, something I loved and longed for and that I believed was good, became for me something to be afraid of and avoided.

Doesn't life have a way of tempting us to stop believing in what is beautiful and good? We end up believing that we are better off dismissing our 'childish' beliefs and our 'naïve' dreams. We start out so free to dream. *So what happens? Where, along the way, did we stop feeling free to dream and believe in the good of things?* But the more important question is *How do we get that freedom back?*

As much as I loved horses, the closest we ever came to owning any were a couple of bouncy horses in the backyard. They were the ones where the horse was attached with springs to a metal frame—very good for galloping long distances. My brother and I would always ride our horses together and we would chant: "Horsey-back-ride, horsey-back-ride, horse-ee-back-ride!" We would repeat this phrase tirelessly and bounce until we were all bounced out.

One morning, we came outside to find that my horse was missing. It was a mystery. Or, as my 3-year-old would say in a whispery, dramatic voice, *it was The Case of the Missing Bouncy Horse.* And so it was. A while after it had gone missing, we were walking up our street one day and we spotted it. It was sitting in my uncle's yard. He lived just up the road from us. He had taken it (stolen it) for his little boy. I was relieved and so happy that we found it. I would get to ride my horse again! Now we could get it back—now all would be well. This seemed the obvious thing to do—to take it back. But this was not the consensus. Naturally, I felt confused when my dad said we would leave it with them. My parents were not going to do anything at all about it. I didn't understand. I felt hurt and even more than that, powerless.

Quite young, I had learned that compliance was the only acceptable response to the decisions my parents made. Any kind of strong objection would be considered disrespectful. The dominating values that governed the atmosphere of our home growing up were: faith in God (my dad was a preacher), obedience, respect for authority, and education.

To be clear, my parents were good-hearted people. Both were likable and well-respected. They were good to us, spent time with us, and passed on to us so many of their values, interests, gifts, and faith. But I don't remember being taught or encouraged as a child to talk through and process my own thoughts and perspective on something. I don't remember there being purposeful inquiry about how this situation, or that event, made me feel. And I don't remember anyone picking me up or crouching down to look me in the eye, wanting to know my heart's response to having my horse stolen.

Let me note here that our experience of the world throughout our childhood *as we perceive it through our child-eyes* is what teaches us about life—it is reality to us. It speaks to us, telling us who we are and how life is. And *our perception* of how things went and why things happened is just as important as whatever other versions of the story there might be, especially within the context of pursuing healing and processing the pain and hurts of childhood and of the past.

A NEW TOWN

The summer that I would turn seven, my dad moved to Pinedale, Wyoming, another small town, about a three-hour drive north of Baggs. Shortly after he left, my mom drove us up to stay with him in a tiny upstairs room of an apartment complex. Later, we would shuffle around until we landed in a two-bedroom apartment.

I was seven when we lived there. I have several pretty clear memories of life in Pinedale. One of the hardest memories I have is of the day my mom left to return to Baggs without us. The plan was for us to stay with my dad while she went back for the rest of the summer to tie up loose ends and to pack up our belongings. Then she would come back, and this would be our new home. As far as I understood it, we were going to stay here, in this new town, in this little apartment, for good. There was no plan to go back. I remember that for as long as we lived in Pinedale, I would think of the white house with black trim. It was still home to me, and I would wish and hope that all of this was a dream, and soon I would wake up from it, back in my own safe bed, in my big, safe house, in my small, familiar town.

This didn't happen of course—at least not in the way I had hoped. On the day my mom was going to leave, I desperately wanted to go with her. I didn't want to stay. I didn't want this to be home. And I didn't want her to leave me behind. I cried and I clung to her legs. I begged and pleaded for her to take me with her, but for many reasons—all grown-up kinds of reasons—she couldn't. I didn't know why she had to go, I just knew I needed to go with her, and maybe if I just begged hard enough and insisted, she would understand how important it was, and maybe then she would change her mind and take me with her. But that didn't happen. She pried me off of her legs, and as she got into the car and drove away, my heart broke. I stood between the curtain and the window and cried, completely powerless to stop this from happening. Not only was my safe, secure world being uprooted, but my mom—a key part of that safe world—would not stay or take me with her, and there was nothing I could do to change that.

After she left I cried a long time. But then I dried my tears; and then, I did what kids do—I adjusted. And as they say, the world kept on turning. That summer we slept late in the mornings and we played a lot. Inside, we played War and Go Fish and Monopoly and Risk and all of the other board games we owned that were popular in the eighties. Outside, we played in the yard with the neighborhood kids and rode our bikes. We ate a lot of lunch meat that summer, and Top Ramen and sour plums.

It was in Pinedale that I started learning to play the piano. I learned fast and I loved to play. I learned a sweet little song called the Reverie Waltz for my first recital. I practiced and practiced, and must have played it a hundred times or more. It lives in my memory today, well beyond any other piece I've ever learned. I don't remember being nervous for that recital, or having any fear at all about playing in front of a crowd. Over time, I came to struggle a lot with performance anxiety, especially whenever I had to play anything from memory. I really grew to dread it.

It is striking how much freedom and courage we actually start out with, and how much of it gets lost. Catching grasshoppers and loving horses and sharing a song are all natural and easy at first, because this is what we were meant to do. We are meant to live without fear. We are meant to love without reserve. And we are meant to share our gifts with others, without apology and without shame. *Is it possible to return to how we were meant to live?*

My parents never really argued in front of us, so it was a surprise to me when my mom brought up the subject of divorce. She and my brother were washing dishes one night, when she posed the question to both of us: "What would you think if your dad and I got a divorce?" Without thinking too much about it, my first thought was, *Hmm. Would I get my own room?* And then of course, I just said that out loud. No filter. My brother was horrified at my question, and he let me know how inappropriate it was in the most exasperated tone, "Chalis! That is not important!" He was only nine at the time, but he understood more than I did.

In the middle of my third-grade year, we stood in the living room of our two-bedroom apartment and said goodbye to my mom. We would return with my dad to live in Baggs, and my mom would stay in Pinedale. I don't remember how I felt as we said goodbye. In fact, my emotions are much stronger now as I write about that moment than they were on that day—at least as far as I can remember. Because now I know what I would face during the months and years that followed. Now I understand how much my heart would hurt those first many months without my mom. Now I know just how great the void would be, when later we were without my dad who lived too far away.

SEPARATED

We spent the rest of that school year, and the next year as well, with my dad in Baggs, back in our big, safe house, back in our small, familiar town. Of course, nothing was the same without Mom. I respect my dad for being the one who cared for us during those first months they were apart. I'm sure the first months must have been difficult for him and it would have been really challenging to care for children while trying to cope with such a painful loss. Our family was broken. We were the new kids in town again. I didn't expect to feel like a new kid there since all I had wanted was to go back to the place I thought of as 'home.' But 'home' is not just a place. 'Home' is where we know we are loved, where we feel safe, where our needs are met, and where all is well with our world. For me, it was my mom and dad, my brother and me, together.

Altogether, my mom was away from us for 18 months, with the exception of a summer visit with her in Florida, and a short winter visit the following Christmas.

During that time, she had gotten remarried. She had moved to Florida, and after we finished school that year, we moved down to live with her. My dad remarried shortly after my brother and I moved to Florida. It was hoped that we would spend every other year living with dad, back and forth, living one year with mom, the next with dad, and so on. But it wasn't realistic for us, and so we ended up living with my mom during the school years and spending the summers with my dad, along with his wife, her son (my stepbrother) and eventually their daughter (my half sister), born during my high school years.

As I am remembering those summer visits, one sweet memory of that time is that every time we went, I would notice and keep being delighted to rediscover all of the little things I had forgotten that reminded me of my happy childhood—by this I mean literally, the 'things,' like the vintage silverware, the eclectic collection of coffee mugs, the cow-head-sippy-straw cups, the knick knacks, the old, ornately carved upright piano, the philodendron that never died, the song the finch sang from his cage, the board games we grew up playing, the dated bureau dresser, and the framed family pictures. Memories of memories.

MY TEENAGE YEARS

Through middle and high school and the years beyond, in many ways, I flourished. I excelled in school; I shone as a leader among my peers; I performed; I made good grades; I read my Bible every day; and above all, I behaved. I always had plenty of approval from the people I needed to please. I was not aware of how much I needed and worked for the approval of other people until much later on, when I wasn't getting it so much anymore. It was the approval of my parents, teachers, and peers that kept me feeling good about myself.

What I was losing through those years was my sense of intrinsic value, my self-worth, my identity, and even my deep-down belief in the goodness and trustworthiness of God. I could never have imagined then what I would much later discover of the anger I held toward God and toward my parents. I was in my mid-twenties before I got my first glimpse of my own brokenness; before I even knew that there was anything going on inside of me that might need some attention.

There is no hierarchy of suffering. There's nothing that makes my pain worse or better than yours, no graph on which we can plot the relative importance of one sorrow versus another.

DR. EDITH EVA EGER

HOLOCAUST SURVIVOR AUTHOR OF
THE CHOICE

The Past

IT IS THE NATURE OF A CHILD TO SOAK EVERYTHING IN, to trust that what he hears and sees is true. Everything that he sees and experiences carries with it a message. And when the message comes, positive or negative, whether through words of praise or criticism, overcoming a challenge, a traumatic experience, an especially memorable moment, or a painful situation, a child naturally receives the message as the truth—about himself, people, God, or life. He tucks it away along with the rest of his growing collection of 'things I know.' As he grows, he carries this collection of messages with him. They become his 'truth,' and form the lens through which he sees and interprets his encounters with others, and everything else he faces in life.

KEY NUMBER 2
ORIGINAL WOUNDS AND THEIR MESSAGES

Negative words or actions, neglect, abuse, hurtful situations, painful circumstances, or even more subtly, feeling overlooked, unseen, or not valued in childhood—all of these, if left to themselves and not resolved, result in wounding a child. This wound creates a 'landing place' so to speak for every situation thereafter that carries a similar message to the message received with the original wound.

Original wounds are deep, and deeply significant, because as children, we do not yet have a foundational set of true beliefs with which to process these wounds and the messages they carry. Our experiences, the good and the bad, are in the very process of shaping and forming our foundational beliefs. In our earliest years, we are still figuring out what's what. What is life about? What is my place in this world? Who can I trust? What do I need to do to get my needs met? The answers we receive to these questions are usually a mixed bag of some truth, some half-truths, and some lies. Whether or not we grew up in the ideal environment, we were all born into an imperfect world, full of sin, loss, pain, and injustice. We cannot escape our earthly reality.

A friend shared a story with me about the grief that surrounded the loss of her 5-week-old baby boy. She and her husband and her three older children had been processing and grieving this deeply painful loss of a child and sibling. Walking together down the sidewalk one day, they saw a parked vehicle that displayed the popular slogan "Life Is Good." Her 4-year-old daughter slowly read the words out loud and then paused a moment. Then she said, "Mommy, sometimes life *isn't* good."

Sometimes, life *isn't* good. Sometimes it is excruciating. There is no one who is exempt from experiencing loss. Ultimately, we cannot control the circumstances we, or our children, will experience. Original wounds can, and will, come from many directions, and when they do, they are aimed at our very essence.

And by the way, our essence, who we are at our core—the Real Me and the Real You—are *vitally important*. The person buried underneath all we have learned to be in order to survive, the person we were originally created to be, the message and the atmosphere we were intended to carry, our unique flavor, the purpose for which we have been born into this world at this particular time in history, is of *paramount significance* because it is an invaluable piece of the story being written of the human race. The Real You is imperative to Our Story.

The World needs the Real You.
There is a part that only the Real You,
Living truly from your heart, can play.
The Real You is irreplaceable.
The Real You is incomparable.
The Real You is made for unimaginable glory.

But it can take some doing to get to the Real. The collective mixture of true and false messages serves to shape our foundational beliefs, which, reinforced and solidified over time, become our Heart Beliefs. We carry these Heart Beliefs into our adulthood, and along the way, now and then, we are presented with opportunities to reevaluate them. Most of us, upon evaluation, will find that we hold at least some *false* Heart Beliefs.

Keep in mind that many of these beliefs are so deeply hidden within us that either we do not realize we harbor them, or we assume that how we think and feel—and deep down believe—is 'just how it is' or 'just the truth.' We must choose whether we might be willing to consider that we do in fact, hold false Heart Beliefs within, and after this, whether or not we will be open to receiving the truth about them through the healing process. Because:

If our beliefs are a result of the messages, and the messages came with the original wounds, it is healing the original wounds of the heart—not changing the mind—that will replace the false

beliefs with the truth, giving us the gift of a clear, truth-based perspective. This new perspective positions us to begin to live a different way, and so to experience life in a whole new way.

KEY NUMBER 3
THE POWER OF ACKNOWLEDGEMENT

There are two ways things can go when we are wronged or experience pain as children. The wrong or the pain is either *acknowledged* by the adults we trust, or for various reasons and not always intentionally, it is *overlooked*.

Acknowledgement helps to develop a healthy, truth-based set of beliefs in the heart of a child. God places us in a family so that when we experience a hurtful situation or wounding words and don't know what to make of it, a parent is able to help us process what we have experienced. If another child says or does something hurtful, a parent can help us to process the hurt and to understand that the words and actions of others do not determine our value or define us. If a parent is impatient or sharp, they can acknowledge their own wrong, apologize, and ask forgiveness. If we experience the loss of a grandparent or a sibling, parents can walk us through the grieving process, helping us to understand our own emotions, and answering questions we might have about death and loss.

In the earliest years, parents are truly a child's world. Parents are a picture to that child of who God is. They are meant to love, to protect, to offer guidance, to provide healthy boundaries, to bring correction, and to instill truth within the heart of that child. The child looks to his parents to provide for his needs. He is one-hundred percent dependent on his parents, and he believes what they teach him. He believes their words, their actions, and their judgments. When a child is wronged and it is overlooked or minimized by the adults he trusts, he is sent the message that what has happened to him is acceptable. The child's sense of self is being formed and shaped in these very moments. He may not consciously think it, but somewhere within him, he believes a lie about himself, "If they are right to hurt me, then something about me must deserve to be hurt. Something about me must be wrong. Something about me is bad." If a child is not taught where the shame belongs, he will take on that shame and carry it within himself.

Something children do intrinsically know is that parents are the ones who, of everyone in the whole world, are meant to love and value them the most. A parent's words, actions, and presence (or absence) in a child's life are truly powerful. This is why being wounded by a parent is such a strong blow to the heart of a child. **For a child to grow up with a healthy, truth-based set of beliefs in his heart, he must grow up in an environment where he consistently experiences a "making right of things."**

Imagine that you are walking through the park, lost in thought. Another person is out for a run, headed your way. He is distracted by something and is looking in another direction, and because you are not paying attention, he ends up running into you, knocking you to the ground. Next, he looks at you for a moment but says nothing—no offer to help you up, no acknowledgement that he has wronged you, and no apology. And then he turns and keeps running. After picking yourself up off the ground, you turn and look after him, now several hundred yards away, and think to yourself, *What in the world?* You feel an indignation rising up. You have been wronged, and it was not made right. *He should have apologized profusely,* you think. *He should have helped me up! Who does he think he is? What a punk.*

Why would this be so disconcerting to most of us? We value justice. We believe that in order to be in right relationship with another person, wrongs must be made right. Offenders must acknowledge their offenses, apologies must be given and accepted, and offenses forgiven.

This scenario would be bizarre to us as adults. Yet many children are consistently treated in ways that violate this law of justice within relationships by the ones who are meant to love them most. When their daily reality is 'twisted' much like the scenario above, their 'lens' or understanding of the world and everything in it becomes a twisted version of reality.

THE TWISTED LENS

This acknowledgement, making things right, is certainly missing in situations of systematic abuse or neglect, or abandonment. But the principle also applies to families where there is dysfunction of any kind, including addictions and enabling behaviors, poor communication, co-dependence, unhealthy boundaries, use of guilt, fear, control, manipulation, or shame, or even just failing to see or pursue a child's heart. A child who has been raised this way becomes an adult whose deeply held false Heart Beliefs have fashioned within him a twisted lens. This twisted lens contorts and changes everything, so that he does not see clearly. Instead, he perceives everything he encounters in a way that can be likened to the hall of mirrors at an amusement park, where each mirror reflects a convoluted, grossly exaggerated image. All of these mirrors reflect the person standing before them, but they do not reflect the reality of the person or their true identity.

The twisted lens distorts our perception of ourselves. The twisted lens can replace healthy self-respect and self-love with self-hatred, false shame, and insecurity. It robs us of a healthy understanding of who we truly are, of our intrinsic worth and our value, of our capabilities, our strengths and weaknesses, and our place in this world. One of my false Heart Beliefs was that I was 'rejectable' and so I often felt rejected by others, even when they were not intending to reject me. Another false Heart Belief I held about myself was 'I must be perfect in order to be loved.' I felt I needed to perform well in school in order to be accepted. I was always trying to please my teachers and my parents, often going above and beyond what was required because I didn't believe that it was enough just to be me. Before I found healing, I desperately needed the approval of others in order to be OK.

I also dealt often with feelings of false shame. As I began the healing process, after some time working with my counselor, I remember waking up one morning and feeling different. It took me a minute to put my finger on it, but after some thought, I realized that this was the feeling of carrying no shame. It was only after I started experiencing this that I realized I had often felt shame upon waking, for no apparent reason, without even really knowing it.

The twisted lens distorts our perception of others. Often as we look at people through this lens, we misjudge their words, motives, and intentions, interpreting their actions through our own set of false Heart Beliefs. For example, if deep down, I hold a false belief that I am inferior because of a poor self-image or shame-based identity, I may perceive another person as being or acting superior even where it may not be the reality; or I might vacillate between feelings of pride and shame, as I constantly compare myself to others, viewing them as above or below me, rather than feeling and believing the truth—that we are all equally significant and equally valuable. In our relationships with others, a twisted lens may cause us to become quick to shut down at the first sign of conflict because deep down, we believe others are going to abandon us; to get defensive at the slightest hint of criticism because deep down, we believe we must be perfect in order to be acceptable and accepted by others; to keep conversation shallow because deep down, I feel that if anyone really gets to know me, they will not like me; to be the one who knows everything because to receive anything (information, instruction, encouragement, counsel) from someone else requires vulnerability, and last time I was vulnerable (childhood) was terrifying/painful/traumatic.

The twisted lens distorts our perception of God. A twisted lens leads us to hold false Heart Beliefs about who and how God is, and about how God sees us as well. It gives us a false understanding of our 'status' in the eyes of God—He calls us *loved*. "For God so loved the world that He gave His only begotten Son, that whoever believes in Him, should not perish, but have everlasting life," (John 3:16).

We really are loved, but we often, deep down, feel that we are hated, forgotten, judged harshly, or that He is ashamed or disappointed with us. I remember one night lying in my bed and through my tears asking God, "Why do you hate me?" It didn't even make sense to me that I was saying it. I knew with my mind that God loved me—I could tell you with words and show you the scriptures all day long. But still, somewhere within me where love should have been, I felt hated, forgotten, and abandoned by God.

This one can be hard for some to see or accept because many have a strong belief in God and would say that God is good and loving, even though they may have experienced something very different with their parents, or with situations or circumstances in their growing up years. Just remember that we are not always aware of our Heart Beliefs. We are aware of what we believe with our mind. Our Heart Beliefs are another matter. For me, it would have been unthinkable to say that I had anger in my heart toward God, or that I didn't trust Him. But when the time came to take a deeper look, I became very honest with myself about how I really felt toward God. And it didn't have much to do with what I knew with my mind.

The twisted lens distorts our perception of life. When as children we suffer abuse, neglect, abandonment, betrayal, trauma, or loss, we take note. We take hold of the messages that accompany these wounds, and we adopt them as the truth about life. Some of them go something like this:

Life is cruel.

If I want anything done right, I have to do it myself.

It is foolish to trust anyone.

Women are manipulative.

Men are selfish and chauvinistic.

If something can go wrong, it will.

Life is hard, and I am on my own.

Others will betray me—every time.

Good things happen for other people, but not for me.

I can never let them see me cry.

The wounds and losses of childhood can rob us of having depth and real connection in our relationships. They can keep us stuck in self-destructive behaviors and they can keep us locked in the self-protection that sabotages the very things we long for in life. Remaining unhealed, they can keep us from really living.

This is why it is so important that we take the time to allow God to guide us into the process of addressing the wounds and losses of our past, with the Holy Spirit counseling and comforting us as we acknowledge and grieve our losses. As He heals us, the wounds and the messages lose the hold they have had on our Heart Beliefs and we are able to begin to really believe and embrace the truth about ourselves, others, God, and life. And as truth brings more and more freedom, we begin to live and experience life in a very different way.

QUESTIONS TO CONSIDER

Can you think of a message you may have received, positive or negative, that came through a situation you experienced as a child?

Thinking back to your childhood, did you have a trusted adult (or adults) in your life who helped you to process things that you experienced?

Would you say you are in agreement with any of the messages in the list above (in the list of false beliefs about life)?

Survival: the act or fact of living or continuing

longer than another person or thing

MERRIAM-WEBSTER

UNABRIDGED DICTIONARY

CHAPTER 7

How We Survived

WE WERE CREATED TO LIVE WITH OUR MIND, WILL, AND emotions operating in sync, so to speak, and in fact, with every aspect of our being—spirit, soul, and body—unified. Yet if you have ever felt divided within yourself about something, you will understand that at times, we know something with the mind, but do not feel it with our emotions. Sometimes we want (will) to be a certain way, or to do a certain thing, but somehow we end up doing the opposite because of a Heart Belief (which is connected to emotion).

When we experience a lack of connection between the different aspects of who we are, we are living with that internal incongruence discussed in chapter one. Our mind is here, our emotions are there, and our will (what we decide to do) is constantly having to choose, divided in its loyalty between the two. The question is, "How did I get this way? What happened to create this 'disconnect' inside of me?" The answer to this question is the fourth KEY I was given, helping me to understand my own heart and my inner condition. It helped me to get my bearings, allowing me to begin to work toward the integration needed to be able to start living from my heart.

KEY NUMBER 4
THE DISCONNECT: SEPARATING FROM MY HEART

We are given the gift of pain as a signal. Pain at touching a hot burner tells us to remove our hand in order to preserve it. Emotional pain for a child signals him to remove himself from the site of the pain (his heart) in order to survive. Yes, children are resilient. Yes, children can adjust/adapt remarkably well, wherever they are. But there is a reason this is so. It is not without cost.

Something significant happens within a child upon receiving the messages that accompany wounds, trauma, or loss, especially when there is no help in processing the situation with a parent or trusted adult. **A child will instinctively remove himself from the landing place of the pain—his core/ his heart —in pursuit of safety, in order to regain a sort of homeostasis for himself.**

And so, as a child retreats from the site of the pain, removing himself from his heart in order to become OK, there comes a split—a separation. There are now two parts of the child:

His Heart, which has now become an unsafe, much too painful place for him to remain; and

His Mask, the alternate, more 'acceptable' version of himself he creates in order to find safety and get his needs met.

Feeling unsafe or insecure, a child will do whatever it takes to ensure his own survival, whether he is working to ensure basic provision (this could happen in cases of severe abuse or neglect), or working to gain love, acceptance, or the attention of a parent. For this reason, a child may learn early on to act in ways that are motivated by a need to please others, to deflect shame, to make people laugh, to show that he is smart, capable, useful, tough, etc., because just being himself (who he is at his core/his heart) proved to be unsafe. He experienced pain as a result of being himself. But putting on a mask and being something other than just himself—here he is safe. Here he can rest assured his needs will be met.

At one point, while I was in the process of learning about this, I saw a picture in my mind of myself as a little girl. In this vision, as I am watching her, it is as if a translucent, sort of holographic little girl steps out and away from herself. As she steps out, she looks back as if to say, 'I'm sorry but I've got to go,' and leaving herself behind, she walks away. As I grew up, this is what I had done—I had left myself—my core/my heart—behind.

When this happens, when we separate from our own heart, we embrace the mask, because the mask seems to serve us so well. Our loyalty is to the mask, and as time goes by, as we grow, and as we make our way into adulthood, we settle into a way of life that feels safe and gives us a sense of control as we work to get our needs met for acceptance, approval, security, and love.

Meanwhile, the heart that we left behind stays young and alone, never growing up. This is why there are parts of most of us that seem to be stuck at a young age. When a situation triggers unhealed wounds in us, we revert back to feeling like the child we were when we first experienced the wounding or the loss. In those places, we may still be 5 years old, or 11 or 14. We will not only *feel* like a child in those moments, but we will react to the situation as a child would.

WHY DO WE DISCONNECT?

Because a child is vulnerable and pure-hearted, it doesn't have to be a traumatic event or abuse that triggers feelings of insecurity. It can be things like being shamed for making mistakes, feeling left out by peers, or being made fun of. It can be that the child's feelings or moods are ignored or overlooked by his or her family, or that their thoughts and opinions are disregarded. The child may all too often be left alone, yet be noticed and praised when he/she brings home good grades or excels at sports. Of course, specific events and losses can also wound us, causing us to seek shelter in the safety of a mask.

My parents' divorce and all that we faced because of it was deeply wounding to me as a child. It was the most significant loss of my childhood, affecting me well into my adult years, and the constant absence of one or the other of my parents from that point forward became my new reality. This was one wound that created for me the need to separate from my heart and live instead out of my mask.

KEY NUMBER 5
SURVIVAL SYSTEMS

With the help of my counselor, the Holy Spirit showed me my survival systems. Survival systems are all of the strategies we use to live out of our mask instead of our true heart, catering to our false Heart Beliefs in order to create for ourselves a safe, non-threatened little world. In this world, our hearts are hidden from view and our needs get met our way. Using survival systems, we are able (so we think) to control our own environment. We work hard to avoid vulnerability by keeping our true selves hidden, and keeping others at a comfortable distance (often all the while wondering why we don't feel close to people).

When we learn to wear masks as children, we eventually find ourselves deeply invested in a number of survival systems without recognizing them for what they are. Some of the common survival systems that we employ are systems of control, performance, contempt, people-pleasing, perfectionism, busyness, care-taking of others, over-attention to outward appearance, judgment/criticism, negativism, addictions, and even spirituality. And this is the short list. (See APPENDIX A for an extensive list of survival systems.)

When a child separates from his or her heart, it can be very subtle. It may even seem like his or her natural strengths are just beginning to shine through. This may also be true, but it is not always easy to know what motivations lay behind the actions. For example, when I was a child, I found out early on that I was able to excel in school, and that I was praised and celebrated for this. It was something I worked at and eventually used as a way to gain approval. I desperately wanted to please my teachers and my parents. I also tried to always do the right thing, not necessarily because it was right, but because I wanted my teachers and parents to see that I was good. I wanted them to look at me and say—there is Chalis. She is always so good. And she sure is smart. She is so helpful. I can trust her. She is my favorite. Even though excelling in school was a natural strength I had as a child, it is easy to see how it could (and did) become a way for me to gain the approval of the adults in my life.

Other ways a child might begin to wear a mask in pursuit of 'safety' might be: not trying at all in school so as not to fail; being silly and funny in order to entertain peers and gain approval while avoiding vulnerability; acting out and getting into trouble on purpose in order to get someone's attention; being 'cool' to gain admiration and acceptance of peers; acting tough and bullying others to cover up feelings of shame and insecurity.

As we grow and progress into adulthood, we experience more and more of life and all of the good and bad of it, much of which only reinforces our perceived need to remove ourselves from the vulnerability of living from our true hearts. We hone our 'survival skills' until we get very good at being something we are not—so good in fact that we ourselves are deceived. The mask we wear and the systems we operate in seem to us to actually be our true self, even though they are not who we are. Living this way for such a long time—for as long as we can remember—we don't really know our own hearts. We don't know who we are at our core because we have only known these systems in order to survive.

Since one of my biggest survival systems was performance, I worked hard to please, going above and beyond, being good at school, being efficient at work, being available whenever there was a need, and so on, to gain acceptance and approval from others.

Even though I struggled a lot with depression through my twenties and into my thirties, I was always functional, because it was performance that provided me with the approval I needed to feel good—kind of like the next 'fix.' I am an introvert by nature. But during those years, finding the acceptance I constantly needed in order to feel OK required being around other people as much as possible, so I filled up my time with social engagements, making sure that I was seldom alone, preferably never. Ironically, the after-effect of social engagements, for me, would often be deep loneliness, because what I was looking for was not at the party, or the concert, or on the date. What I was looking for I would find much later—drinking coffee in my PJ's, hanging out with my own heart and Jesus.

RECOGNITION

Who remembers a running GI Joe commercial growing up that would teach safety tips for children? They always ended with the child saying "Now I know!" to which the GI Joe character would reply "and knowing is half the battle!"

One of the biggest obstacles to our healing is a denial of the possibility that we are operating in unhealthy ways. We can believe that we are doing great holding it all together, while the reality is that we are steeped in our survival systems, giving us the *illusion* that everything is under control.

But knowing is half the battle! If there is a willingness to know, a simple prayer will suffice. Ask for revelation of any survival systems you may be operating in unknowingly. God is always willing to reveal truth, if we are willing to hear it, in order to move us toward His true healing and wholeness.

QUESTIONS TO CONSIDER

Can you think of one or more example(s) of how the different aspects of your personhood (spirit, soul, and body; or mind, will, and emotion) may not be operating in unity?

Consider your daily life. Do you feel any measure of disconnect between how you feel on the inside, and your life (what others see) on the outside?

Take some time to search the extended list of Survival Systems in APPENDIX A. Are there any areas that seem to be highlighted as you read the list? Make a list of any survival systems that you think might be at work in your life.

Where there is sorrow there is holy ground.

Some day you will realize what that means.

You will know nothing of life till you do.

OSCAR WILDE

DE PROFUNDIS AND
OTHER PRISON WRITINGS

CHAPTER 8

At the Crossroads

FOR MANY YEARS, MY MOODS WERE ALWAYS CONTINGENT upon circumstance. When things were good, I felt good. When nothing good or exciting was happening, I felt bad. When I felt bad, I would call my mom, because my mom was my biggest cheer-leader. She was my tried and true, best, reliable source for words of affirmation, on demand. She always picked up the phone, and she always dropped whatever she was doing, and told me all the good things about me. If there was a conflict, she would show me all the reasons I was right, and the other person was wrong. And to be honest, this worked pretty well for me for a long time.

This was how I lived. As time went on, my mom was the one who finally pointed out to me one day how often I was depressed. I got frustrated with her for saying so, and I reminded her that I only called her when I was feeling bad, so *of course* she would think that I was always feeling bad. This was true, but how often did I call her?

I'm sure out of concern and probably feeling at a loss for how else to help me, her last-ditch effort that day was to tell me to "just snap out of it." She said I could change my mind about how I was going to feel—that I got to *choose* how to feel. This was unbearably annoying for me to hear. Inside, I was a five-year-old with my hands clapped over my ears singing: *oh when the saaaaints... go marching iiin....*

Even though she was right about how often I was depressed, informing me of it did not help. I was not quite at the end of my rope yet, and I didn't trust her counsel. Shortly after this conversation, I ended up reconnecting with an old friend from college. I recklessly made the decision, after not too many months, to marry him. And silly me, I thought this would be a Once In A Lifetime thing, so I planned the picture-perfect, way-too-expensive, wedding-of-my-dreams wedding, and invited everyone I knew.

I might have known something was awry when, on our honeymoon (an Oregon road trip planned with his pot-farming aspirations in mind) he got angry with me (I can't remember the reason) and punished me with silence, freezing me out for *thirty hours straight*—I know this because I made sure to calculate it. This was just one of several hard and often confusing conflicts that took place over the course of our week-long road trip. Unfounded accusations, heated, 'crazy-making' arguments, a cold and absolute absence of empathy. My lack of foresight and the lack of wisdom that had guided this decision were becoming more apparent as the week progressed, and a sinking feeling of regret set in very near the beginning of everything. But I wanted to believe that it was just what happens when you get married. Everyone argues, right? Everyone has challenges and disagreements, right?

Returning from our trip, the conflict continued. The arguments were heated and they seemed to be getting worse, and the confusing way they were being instigated was keeping me in turmoil. It was wearing me down, and it was demoralizing. Somewhere in all of it, my self-image had reached an all-time low.

Several weeks into it, I was sitting with my mom one day, and as we talked, she was trying to encourage me. "Everybody fights. It can be hard in the moment, but when you are married to a good man, and you love each other, you can work it out." I looked up through my tears and shook my head slowly as I said, "Mom, he's not a good man."

A very good friend, who was a mental health counselor, voiced her concern after listening to my stories. Things continued to escalate, and so with the support and counsel of my friend, as well as my family, I moved out of the house just six weeks after we said 'I do' and by the following September, we were divorced.

Dream shattered. This was my greatest failure to date. The picture I had of 'how things were supposed to go' was destroyed. I became very raw. I started feeling less and less tolerant of everything—of running into people I knew, making small talk, being in crowds, being with friends, and being alone.

The weeks and months that followed our separation were dark. Making final decisions and settling things required encounters or correspondence that usually made me feel sick to my stomach. I was angry with myself for the decisions that had led me here. Most of these days were full of tears and confusion, and asking questions, but getting no answers. Inside, I carried a deep sense of failure, shame, and regret. What I had thought I wanted more than anything, had finally happened for me. Yet it was never love, and it held no trace of what I needed or longed for. It held the appearance of love, and it presented itself as the picture I had painted, promising 'happily ever after,' but it was not based in reality, and it did not deliver.

PART III

Where Do We Go From Here?

There is a time for everything, and a season for

every activity under heaven:

a time to be born and a time to die,

a time to plant and a time to uproot,

a time to kill and a time to heal,

a time to tear down and a time to build,

a time to weep and a time to laugh,

a time to mourn and a time to dance,

a time to scatter stones and a time to gather them,

a time to embrace and a time to refrain,

a time to search and a time to give up,

a time to keep and a time to throw away,

a time to tear and a time to mend,

a time to be silent and a time to speak,

a time to love and a time to hate,

a time for war and a time for peace.

ECCLESIASTES 3:1-8

CHAPTER 9

Supplies

THE HEALING JOURNEY LOOKS DIFFERENT FOR EVERYONE.
I spent time in counseling on and off throughout my twenties with
various counselors and found that only a fraction of that time
resulted in any measure of healing or real change. But coming to
my lowest point, I believe now that God was waiting for me to get
to a place where I was no longer tied to anything I thought I knew.
Leading up to that time, as I shared in chapter two, I had been
questioning everything, and had in fact, become deeply disillu-
sioned in terms of my faith, which was a big part of my identity.
The divorce was just the final confirmation that my life was not
working. I was raw, and I was tired of trying to keep it all together.
And this was a very good place to be. Here, there was room for Him
to move. He had my attention. I was more pliable and more willing
to do whatever I needed to do, and I was no longer worried about
disappointing anyone.

Once I started meeting with my counselor on a regular basis,
things really began to move. There were a few 'essentials' that saw
me through this process.

A COUNSELOR

I always say I wish everyone could see Pat (my counselor). But everyone can't see Pat. But everyone *can* find a counselor. First, through prayer, we can ask God and believe He will lead us to a counselor who will be able to walk with us as we pursue our healing. Talking to friends, contacting local churches, and checking online, a name or even a counseling center or program may be highlighted for you to connect with. It is a good idea to contact potential counselors to find out what their general approach is with their clients. Look for a counselor whose approach is focused on addressing root issues. The list of resources I have included in APPENDIX C may also be helpful. God wants to bring healing, and He is able to bring the right people into our lives in order to accomplish this.

A TRUSTED, SAFE FRIEND

Even before I began seeing my counselor, God brought two friends into my life that became key people in my healing process. I felt impressed that for that season, I was meant to eliminate the time I had been investing in nearly all of my other relationships. It became a season of solitude for me. Besides work and church and occasionally seeing my family, my contact with the outside world consisted of meeting with my counselor, or meeting one of these two friends. The rest of the time was me and Jesus at home, alone.

Since I only saw my counselor once a month, it was pretty important for me to be able to talk and process much of what I was going through with someone else who was on the same page. Though solitude may be an important aspect of this pursuit, having someone, like a close friend, to process with and even to cry with is just as important. Consider inviting a friend or a mentor to go through this book with you, or to let you share with them and process what you are finding as you go.

TIME ALONE

As I mentioned above, time alone was one of my biggest commodities. At times I hated it because loneliness was one of my greatest struggles. But I was also thankful for it because it was an invaluable part of my healing. As I continued through the process, which included a lot of writing, praying, thinking, and grieving, I eventually found peace with it because I knew that the time had been a gift to me, and that I would never have that much time again. I also knew that it was part of why I was able to move so quickly (it only took a few years!) through the most intense stretch of my healing journey, and forward into a fresh new season of seeing many of my deepest lifetime longings fulfilled.

Not only did it give me ample time and space to process and to grieve the losses of my childhood, it served as a constant 'set-up' for me ('set-ups' will be discussed in chapter 10), forcing me to face my fears, my loneliness, and my disappointed longings.

Pat would always tell me, "It's much easier to pursue healing when you are single than when you are married," and now I see how right she was. I am married now with two small children, and time alone is precious—and rare. Especially time alone at home (where I can let myself cry if I want to).

If time alone is rare for you, pray that God will open the door for you to be able to find that time. See if there are ways to eliminate some things from your schedule. Look for creative ways to be alone. It may mean driving to a lake or a park and sitting in your car while you hash something out with God or revisit a painful memory. Quite often, my car was my best alone space. I lived in a little apartment at the time so I didn't feel free to raise my voice or make any loud noise. But driving down the freeway one night, I found a voice for the anger I didn't know I had toward God, and I just let it all go! I had not even been aware how much anger had been buried inside.

A JOURNALING SYSTEM

I have kept a journal from the time I was about 13 years old. The first few journals I filled were just thin, spiral notebooks, and in them, I would write, "Dear Diary..." It must have been in college or so that when I found and reread them, I was so mortified at the thought of anyone ever reading them that I couldn't get them in the trash fast enough! I continued to keep my journals in spiral notebooks until eventually, I started using pretty decorative journals that I would receive as gifts. When I began this season of healing in my mid-thirties, I felt impressed at one point that I should read through all of my journals one last time before burning them. I wanted to burn them because to me, they represented the past and the way I used to be. It was symbolic for me to be able to process and then release it all, because for most of my life, I had been in the habit of holding onto the past. I started from the earliest journal and read chronologically through every page I had written. It was not easy. It was at times boring and it was frequently embarrassing, but here and there, it was inspiring. It was a very good exercise because it brought me back into the emotions of the drama that had been my life; except this time, with some understanding of the unhealthy systems I had lived with. It allowed me to re-process things, bringing closure to many of the hurtful or disappointing situations and relationships that had colored my memories and had contributed to the shame, self-hatred, and depression I dealt with. I can't remember how long it took—I want to say it was several months before I was able to burn the last of my 'before' journals.

As for my healing season, once I began to process things, I began to have much more to write than I ever had before. Writing was making a way for the voice of my heart to be heard. My hand could not keep up with my heart—there was too much to say! It became a priority for me to find a way to journal faster, so I started journaling on my computer. One month (I remember that it was the month of

July) I wrote about 30,000 words. My poor little keyboard got a good workout! And I have never gone back to a handwritten journal.

I have read that there are important connections and different flavors of creativity happening in the brain when one writes with the hand versus typing on a keyboard, so for this reason, some might prefer to stick to a handwritten journal. Whatever helps you to look forward to being alone with your heart—do it. There is no right or wrong, but it is pretty important to find a way to get your thoughts down.

Besides journaling, there are many other ways to process things. You may find yourself putting the voice of your heart to words by some other means of expression. It may be that you are able to find that voice through writing a song, or painting a picture, or it may be a combination of expressing your heart through your gifts, and then writing about that experience. You may like to plant flowers, take pictures, run, play an instrument, cook, etc.—whatever you love. One friend who was pursuing her own healing talked about how she loved greeting cards, and that one day as she stood reading greeting cards, she found one that expressed exactly how she felt about her own heart—so she bought herself that card. I thought that was beautiful!

GIVING MY HEART PRIORITY

There was a period of time that I was desperate enough for healing and change to make the decision that I would give my own little girl (my heart) first dibs on my time and attention. Before this, I had always put everything and everyone else before her. I never felt free to say no to people, so I was always doing things she didn't really want to do. I would spend my time with people she didn't really want to be with out of obligation, or to avoid hurting someone's feelings (but disregarding hers). I would neglect her nutritional needs, eating cereal for dinner, yet making sure I was always stocked with my favorite comfort foods and drinks. I would fill my time with almost anything just to escape her company.

Making the decision to give my little girl priority, I learned that saying yes to my own heart would require choosing often to say no to other people (quite a challenge for me), disappointing people, turning down invitations and opportunities that I was tempted to accept; it would require turning off the TV, resisting a glass of wine or a bowl of ice cream; it would mean sitting still and letting myself feel and face loneliness instead of trying to escape it.

I also learned not to do things with or for people out of feeling like I *should*. I learned how to wait and find out what my heart wanted or needed, and then to follow that voice, rather than the voices of everyone around me, or my own need to please them. My counselor would talk about putting her own name on her calendar so that if someone asked her to do something at that time, she would say she couldn't because she had already scheduled someone else there—herself!

Giving my own heart priority was no small sacrifice. Many of my relationships were strained, some even set aside for a period, because of the changes I was making as I chose to put my own heart and my own need for healing first. It was hard for me to know that I might seem selfish or appear to lack compassion for others, but I was fighting for my heart. I was also learning that sometimes my 'no' was actually good for the other person, making a way for them to face their own issues, or for another person's 'yes' to be possible.

PREPARATIONS

Even though there is no one prescription or one right way to pursue healing, getting these things in place is kind of like buying new school supplies at the beginning of the year: I kind of dread it, but also kind of exciting! Making preparations to pursue our healing can be a sort of preparation of the heart. It can demonstrate to ourselves that we are making a commitment to pursue healing, and are allowing God the freedom to direct our path in order to bring change and freedom as we co-labor with Him in fighting for our hearts.

QUESTIONS TO CONSIDER

Pray and ask for direction in choosing the people you might want to approach for counseling, mentorship, or friendship as you set out on your healing journey.

Consider your typical daily or weekly schedule. Is there time and space in your schedule for you to be able to spend some 'alone time' on a regular basis? If not, think about how you might be able to make some changes in your schedule. If you live with a spouse or a family, it may be helpful to communicate your need to them and see if together, you can figure out how you might have some 'alone time' at home each week. If this is impossible, think about some alternative ways to get alone in order to pray and process things.

When we begin to make our own heart a priority, we usually find that the changes we are making can cause disappointment for those around us, especially if they have been accustomed to us saying 'yes' in the past. Saying 'yes' to my own heart often requires saying 'no' to others. What feelings arise as you anticipate the possibility of causing others disappointment?

*What are my disowned feelings? They are like
strangers living in my house invisible except for
the food they steal, the furniture they leave out
of place, the mud they trail down the hall.*

You can't heal what you can't feel.

DR. EDITH EVA EGER

HOLOCAUST SURVIVOR AUTHOR OF
THE CHOICE

CHAPTER 10

Emotions and Set-ups

EMOTIONS

EVEN THOUGH WE HAVE BEEN CREATIVELY DESIGNED TO experience a wide range of emotions, most of us have become so disconnected from our hearts that we often have a hard time identifying the specific emotions that we're feeling or harboring. Not only this, when we do recognize a specific emotion, it may actually be an emotion that is linked to our survival systems, rather than the underlying emotions of our true heart. Below are two scenarios that illustrate this:

SCENARIO #1

Leslie is in a good mood because she is having a productive day at work, and is feeling <u>cheerful</u> and <u>enthusiastic</u> toward others. However, looking deeper, we would find that underneath she often struggles with feeling <u>less than</u>, <u>worthless</u>, and <u>insecure.</u> Because of this, she is *compelled and driven to produce* so that her co-workers and her boss will see and appreciate her for what she does. This is important because their recognition makes Leslie feel <u>capable</u>, <u>noticed</u>, <u>significant</u>, and <u>accomplished</u>. Not only that, but earning an upcoming promotion will mean having more influence (so she will feel <u>heard</u>), more authority (so she will feel <u>powerful</u>), more respect (so she will feel <u>respected</u>), and more security (so she will feel <u>safe</u> and <u>in control</u>).

This scenario paints a picture of someone who is steeped in a system of performance. To ask her on this particular day, Leslie can recognize and tell you that she feels positive and cheerful. Yet searching deeper, we see that she feels the need to prove herself at work, which temporarily assuages feelings of worthlessness and insecurity, and that she is compelled to perform well in order to gain a sense of significance, power, and respect. Somewhere within, Leslie has felt insignificant, powerless, and disrespected. She needs to be heard and seen, so she has probably felt unheard or unseen at some point along the way.

When our hearts feel heard, seen, significant, empowered, and respected, we are no longer driven to search or grasp for these things at all cost. From this place of security, we are free to say no when we need to say no, to rest when we need to rest, to be OK when we need to leave something undone for a time. And rather than feeling 'less than' we feel 'just as much as' anyone else (no more, no less). We feel our worth. We feel secure.

SCENARIO #2

Andy has always struggled to maintain any close friendships because whenever anyone starts to get too close, something happens—usually a conflict. Every time a conflict arises, his <u>anger</u> flares up. He blows up, and usually ends up walking out on the other person. Afterwards, he stews over it, justifying himself and blaming the other person, and is unable to ever really apologize or forgive, so friendships never seem to last past the first conflict. Searching a bit deeper, we would learn that Andy has a shame-based identity. Deep down, he does not want anyone to know him because he believes that when they really get to know him, they will not like him. After every conflict, he feels <u>ashamed</u> and <u>embarrassed</u> about how he has behaved. He feels <u>angry</u> with himself for not being able to control his temper. But he also feels a strong need to be right for <u>fear of being wrong (imperfect)</u>, and he has a deep <u>fear that he may be exposed or thrown away</u>. Being the first to walk away is his self-protection, and saves him from the potential pain of rejection.

In this scenario, the emotion Andy could probably tell you about is anger. He most likely doesn't know that he is operating in the survival systems of anger, blame, and excusing, rather than taking responsibility. He probably doesn't recognize the emotions underneath of shame and self-hatred, or the fear of being exposed, rejected, or thrown away.

Many of our survival systems make it difficult to recognize our emotions. Some of these systems include false positivity, spiritualizing everything, escaping through fillers like alcohol, food, sweets, TV, social media, etc., contempt of self or others through sarcasm or humor, excusing instead of facing truth, false strength, or learned helplessness (victim), and there are many more. It may be necessary to first identify some of our survival systems so that we are able to make a conscious effort to stop short when we find ourselves going to those places, and by doing so, make space for the true emotions of our heart to rise to the surface and be made known—to ourselves!

When we have spent years or for some, decades, of our lives disregarding or pushing down or covering up our emotions—which we do when we are living disconnected from our hearts—it can be difficult to recognize what we are feeling once we do start to take a look at our inner life. For me, whenever conflict would come or any situation would arise that touched unhealed places within, I would simply shut down. Looking back now, I believe that this was the reason I walked away from many potentially good relationships in my twenties and thirties. Yet I would often wonder why I was not 'finding anyone,' even though I wanted very much to get married and have a family.

My husband, Shane, pursued me for a few years before we actually got together. We had both been going through counseling separately for most of that time, needing to deal with many past issues and wounds before we could really see each other or love each other in a healthy way. We did not purposely wait for our healing before we started dating. Yet until many of our issues from the past were addressed, the two of us together just wouldn't work. He was too over-the-top for me, and I was not interested! Eventually, he came to a place of relaxing and being my friend without expecting anything, and I came to be able to trust, and to take a risk. I found myself thinking about him one day, but with a different feeling than I usually had toward him, and I was surprised that I was opening my heart to him! It was only once we both found a certain measure of healing that it was possible for us to relate to each other out of a place of seeing, appreciating, and valuing each other, rather than needing or even using one another. We entered into the relationship connected to our own hearts, rather than being disconnected, so we were able to process our conflicts and issues, each making an effort to see the heart of the other when disagreements would arise.

This was not necessarily automatic, either—I still found myself, especially in the beginning, shutting down and preparing to walk away several times; but when I recognized it as a sign that there were underlying emotions that needed to be dealt with, I would (with some difficulty) stop myself. At first, I couldn't just come out with what was going on inside, because I didn't always know yet;

but I could at least stay put. Instead of becoming angry or defensive or 'over it,' Shane would recognize when I was shutting down and would begin to gently ask me the right questions so that I was able to identify the emotions I was experiencing in response to our conflict that were causing me to shut down. Once I could identify and share them, the walls of defense would come down, and as I was able to process my emotions with him, each time I would trust a little bit more. I was learning slowly that this was a safe person, and that I did not have to fear that he would abandon me. He was showing me that not only could he be trusted to stay; he could be trusted with my heart. He saw and cared for my heart. In this way, our relationship began to be a safe, healing place for me.

My counselor always says, "Emotions are the voice of our hearts." **Taking the time to identify what kinds of emotions are being evoked within us is a vital part of pursuing our own hearts because often, the intensity of the emotion we are experiencing in a conflict or a difficult situation originates with the wounds of our childhood, rather than the present situation.** I may be facing a situation that reminds me somewhere inside that I have been here before ... I have felt this before, I have heard this message before, I have felt this pain. And when this happens, it is as though I am back in that moment—that moment of helplessness, powerlessness, fear, pain, loneliness, or feeling unseen—and so, even though I am a 'grown-up,' in *this* moment, *I am that child.* In the present, my heart is feeling what that little girl felt, because my heart *is still that little girl.*

If we are not willing to consider and explore this (however silly it may feel for some), our hearts continue to be young and immature in all of the places we have been wounded, and so we will continue to face the same scenarios and outcomes time after time. Through my emotions, my heart is crying out, "Please see me! I feel _____ (lonely, afraid, helpless, terrified), and I really need your attention!" When I choose not to acknowledge the cries of my heart by giving time and priority to my emotions, then I am saying to my own heart, "No, I will not look at you. You are not important to me. You do not matter."

There is a difference between being *ruled* by our emotions (not a good practice, and not the goal here) and *acknowledging* and *exploring* our emotions as a way to see, hear, and validate our own hearts. Basing all of my decisions on my feelings and whims (flakiness), or flying off the handle (a 'grown-up' temper tantrum) whenever something angers me, for example, are immature, unhealthy behaviors. But acknowledging and exploring my emotions as they arise in challenging situations is a necessary part of the healing process and begins to carve out a pathway toward the 'treasures of darkness' within (Isaiah 45:3).

As a place to start, and for a reference, a list of negative emotions can be found in APPENDIX B.

SET-UPS

OK, so I have made the brave decision that I am willing to do whatever it takes to pursue my own heart—even if that means choosing to look at difficult, painful emotions. Now what? The great thing about this process is that we don't have to do much to get things rolling. If now is the time for healing, the set-ups will come.

What are set-ups? **Set-ups are situations or circumstances that elicit within us an over-reaction, or an exaggerated emotional response.** They are things that push our buttons, so to speak. When something happens or someone says something and I find myself reacting with an exaggerated, even irrational set of emotions in response, I am probably experiencing a set-up. We may need to keep our eyes open and look a bit more closely at some of our situations, because for most of us, we are so used to reacting a certain way to things, we probably don't recognize our emotions as being exaggerated or irrational—we can think "It's how anyone would respond!" Be open to the possibility that it isn't. Set-ups are great because they are a starting place. Once we can recognize that we have been set up, it's off to the races.

What is really happening during a set-up? Remember that when we have been wounded, we are living and walking around still wounded, and we carry the messages that accompany those wounds with us. We are operating out of many of the false beliefs held deeply within us without realizing it. We are seeing the world through a twisted lens.

When something happens that seems to confirm the message of a childhood wound, it acts as an arrow to pierce that unhealed wound. Just as a fresh blow would cause acute pain in an unhealed physical wound, a fresh arrow of pain in the present will reopen and exacerbate the pain of the original emotional wound. This is why we may react to the present situation in an exaggerated or irrational way—because we are actually feeling and responding to the pain of the original wound.

I will share an example. One of the things I would sometimes struggle with was a sense of feeling left out, and a longing to belong. When I set out to purposefully explore this emotion, I was able to trace it back to a painful experience I had as a little girl. When I was four or five years old, my dad was a part of a men's community softball league, and we would often walk the few blocks down the street to the softball fields to watch the games. One day, as my mom and I made our way up the bleachers, there were four little girls wearing brand new matching cheerleading uniforms, lined up in front of the fence, clapping and cheering and watching the game together. When the team would get a run, they would count off and begin to recite a cheer they had rehearsed. I knew them well, because our families were friends. As I watched them cheering together, making their motions in unison, my heart ached with wishing I had been invited, and as we set out for home, the tears came quickly. I learned that day what it feels like to be overlooked, and to feel left out.

Remember also that the point of the original wound is the point where we separated from and left our hearts behind. My heart (my little girl) is still right where I left her, so a set-up will take me back to where she still is—back to her emotion in that moment. Every set-up is creating an opportunity for me to revisit and relive the emotions she felt then, and continues to feel again and again every time the unhealed wound is touched in the present.

What do we do with a set-up? When a set-up comes, we can begin to ask some important questions. The first step, though, is to ask the Holy Spirit to lead and counsel us as we explore this, looking for any deeper issue that may need attention.

Here is where writing is a really helpful tool in this process. When we begin to ask questions and write down the answers, often, one thought will lead to another, which leads to another, and another, and so on. This leads us into deeper waters—allowing us to discover more of the less obvious things like underlying motives, hurts, longings, disappointments, anger and the emotions underneath it, needs, etc. In processing through writing, we are navigating the deep waters in a safe way. We can often write what we will not or cannot say out loud. It allows us to take our time. We are able to stop and think, to feel, and to allow ourselves to cry (an important expression of grief) without inhibition.

QUESTIONS TO ASK WITH A SET-UP

Thinking about a situation in your life that has brought up a strong emotional reaction within you, or caused you to 'shut down,' ask yourself the following questions, taking as much time as you may need to thoroughly answer them in writing:

1. What emotion(s) was I feeling during this situation? What emotion(s) have I felt afterward, whenever I think about what happened? (Use the Negative Emotions list in APPENDIX B to help answer these questions with specific, rather than general, descriptive words.)
2. When did I experience these emotions as a child? What was the situation? How old was I?
3. What message did that experience (wound) send to me? Deep down, have I believed this message to be true?

These questions are really just foundational, beginning questions that are meant to help us explore set-ups. What to do with the answers to these questions is coming up. In chapter twelve, we will talk about our role in re-parenting the little boy or little girl of our childhood, bringing truth to replace many of the lies we have believed, and allowing the wounds of childhood to be healed, so that we might begin to grow up in those places and start living free from the pain of our past.

QUESTIONS TO CONSIDER

If you were able to recognize some of your own survival systems in answer to the last question at the end of chapter seven, take another look at the list you made. Take some time and try to identify at least one emotion that may be getting covered up by one or more of the survival systems on your list.

Take a few minutes to briefly consider the many aspects of your life presently: your family, your work, your home life, your responsibilities, your fears or worries, your hopes and dreams for the future. Now with all of this in mind, ask your heart, "How are you feeling right now, in this moment?" It can help to close your eyes and just allow your heart some time to answer. Try to think of two positive and two negative descriptive words. Use the list in APPENDIX B if needed, to get specific.

Can you think of a situation, recent or otherwise, that has been a set-up for you, though you may not have realized it at the time? How did you respond to the situation? What emotions did you experience?

He heals the brokenhearted

and binds up their wounds.

PSALM 147:3

CHAPTER 11

Three Healing Years

IT WAS THROUGH A SERIES OF DIVINE CONNECTIONS AND appointments that I came to a healing place—by this I mean a literal place—where I met my friend, Nicole, and my counselor, Pat. The first experience I had of this healing place was at a Thursday night worship session I had been invited to. There were three people in the room that night: two guys were playing guitars, one of them was singing; a girl was sitting in a back-row seat, journaling. The girl greeted me warmly, and then continued with her journaling. I pulled out my own journal, and I began to draw. I wrote down some thoughts, some words, and I was just taking it all in. As I listened to the music, I felt like God had just brought me here to sing to me. I was enthralled with the beauty of the music. It was simple, it didn't have a lot of words, and it was so gentle, like a soft, cool, ocean wave, like a comforting balm. At first, I wondered who had written it because it seemed to me to be the most beautiful song I had ever heard. But the more I listened, the more I started to realize that it was not a song anyone had written down. It was not a song anyone had carefully crafted. It was a spontaneous song.

It had just bubbled up, out of the spirit of the one who sang it, and it just rose up as an offering to the Lord, not captured, not recorded, just offered up and released. And I never heard the song after that because it had been spontaneous, but I remember the moment of it—the experience of something I would embrace wholeheartedly, and that would become an important part of my healing journey.

Spontaneous, prophetic worship was something that was a brand-new thing for me in those years, and it was incredibly healing for me to sit there among the sounds and rhythms of heaven, crying, or praying, releasing the cries of my heart. I loved this new experience of spontaneous worship so much because I always felt like God was the One writing the songs. Like no man gets the credit for this—this in itself was like a salve to me. And much of the time, the music was both filling me up and washing me off, like I was standing in the flow of a river, and it was washing over all the 'things of earth' so that they grew dim, and the light of Jesus grew very bright and close and present. And in those times, I could become very present, very aware of the moment with Him, and I could just sit and soak in that moment. Here in these moments, He was 'restoring unto me the joy of His salvation.' (Psalm 51:12) Where disillusionment had torn so much away in so many ways, being in His presence so tangibly in these times, He was wooing me with Rememberings. He was bringing back to my mind and my heart all the reasons I had chosen to follow Jesus way back in the beginning, as a little girl; all the true and good things about knowing and believing that Jesus loves me, and that He died on a cross so that I could live with Him forever.

So this place became my 'church' even though at that time, it did not call itself a church. This place was where I spent my Sunday mornings and my Thursday nights, and whatever else came up that drew me there. It was where I sat through services weeping whenever things moved me, and most things moved me in those years;

it was where I would go to meet with my counselor; it was where I showed up to play and sing; and it was where I learned things I had never known about the Holy Spirit. It was where I met some of the people who are my closest friends today, and where I reconnected with the man that I am married to today.

What did those days look like? It was a memorable season because it was such a pivotal time in my life. I would meet with my counselor once a month, and I would meet my friend Nicole for breakfast every Tuesday morning. I would never wear makeup to my counseling sessions with Pat, because it would all get completely washed off about twenty minutes in, so why bother? I would use up half a box of tissues every time I went. I would show up, sometimes with specific things I wanted to talk about, and other times, not. There was usually some kind of bothersome interaction or offense I'd taken with someone, but there was always background information that was needed to set the stage, so I would start with that, thinking it was like a warm-up, like a pre-story. I would get about three lines into the pre-story, and Pat would interrupt me. She would completely ignore whatever I was saying about the other person (who was about to be clearly in the wrong, see?) and instead, she would hone in on *me* and *my* thinking and *my* response and *my* emotions about it, and 'was there a time when you can remember feeling this way in the past?' Her interruptions would always derail my story, and more times than not, we never got to the actual thing I came prepared to talk to her about. Grrr! This was challenging, although it's funny to me now, but it is also why my life was completely changed. Because this wise woman was not interested in being a 'yes-person' in my life; she was not concerned with what the other guy was doing; she was challenging me to look at my own stuff, and do something about it. And this was love.

My job in these sessions was to let her interrupt me; to accept words that were hard to hear and to choose to fully receive them;

to trust that she knew more than I did; to let myself be wrong about things; to cry when my heart needed to cry; to be willing to imagine myself as a little girl, even when it felt stupid or silly; to just let go of control; to stop needing to be right all the time; to admit my own weakness, be OK with my imperfection, and allow myself to be needy.

Meeting with my friend Nicole was kind of like meeting with Pat, only we ate bacon-egg-n-cheese croissants (also sometimes scones) and drank coffee while we talked, and I only cried about half as much because we were usually sitting in a cafe—very public.

And the rest of the time, the rest of the days in between, I would spend whatever time I could, praying, reading, journaling, and grieving. I was learning during this time, what it felt like when I was experiencing a set-up. I was learning to identify specific emotions that were coming up, and to think about why I might be having an exaggerated, emotional response to a situation; I was beginning to look back and identify some of my unhealthy thinking patterns and false Heart Beliefs. For three years, I spent as much time as I could, getting to know myself, and allowing God to show me all of the crooked places within me. And sometimes the loneliness was unbearable. And sometimes the grief felt like it would swallow me up. And sometimes I didn't know if I was ever going to stop crying.

But I did stop crying. I mean technically, I still indulge in a good, ugly cry from time to time, but this full-on Three Years of Tears, did finally start to dry up.

My favorite part of the story is that shortly after I became aware that the season was finally changing for me, I also felt like something had shifted in my heart. I was ready to love and be loved—for real this time. Three years after my first counseling appointment, down to the month, my heart started to become open toward the man that I would eventually marry, and today, we are married with two beautiful children.

Weeping may endure for a night,

but joy comes in the morning.

PSALM 30:5

CHAPTER 12

Pursuing My Heart: The Process

NOW WHEN I THINK OF ALL OF THE YEARS I WAS DISCONNECTED from my heart, I picture a little girl who, knowing she had been left behind, watched and waited for me as I lived out of my mask, trying to make my life work. When, as an adult, I was faced with hurts, disappointments and failures, my anger and contempt would be directed at her. I would blame her, shame her, and reject her, and it was this rejection—*my own rejection of her*—that was hurting her and causing her pain over and over again.

It is important to note that we do again and again to our own hearts what was done to us. Until we make the decision to pursue healing, we perpetuate the cycle of rejection or betrayal or abandonment that keeps us trapped in our own cages and living wounded.

Even though I would shed many tears over these years, they were not healing tears because I was not grieving my true losses. When in the present I was losing a relationship, a dream, a position, an image, I cried, believing that I was losing out because of my own unworthiness. The present losses always seemed to be confirming my false Heart Belief that I was intrinsically inadequate. I was shedding tears in agreement with all of the lies that called my heart rejectable, unworthy of love, shameful, not enough, or too much. My counselor would call these 'tears unto death' because they did not lead to healing or life. Believing these lies about myself kept me from enjoying and loving my life and my own company, and from being able to be myself with other people.

I was feeling this little girl's sadness (my own heart's sadness), but my tears were misplaced. What was she sad about? She was sad because instead of seeing her, I was rejecting her. The present losses would touch the unhealed places, and I would experience the pain of past wounds. The intensity of emotion was my heart's way of trying to bring the need for healing to my attention. It was as though a little girl was standing next to me, tugging on my skirt. And what does a child need? She needs for me to turn and give her my attention, to crouch down to her level and look into her eyes. She needs for me to acknowledge her tears, to find out where her sadness is coming from, and then to take the time to deal with it on her behalf. She needs for me to speak up for her. And then she needs for me to scoop her up and squeeze her tight and tell her how much I love her. Her needs and her longings have always been for love and acceptance—from me.

ADVOCATING FOR MY HEART

Walking through the healing process, our job becomes to re-parent our own little girl or little boy. This time around, I have the chance to give her what every child deserves to have. *I* get to be the one to advocate for her where she has been wronged, acknowledging the injustices against her, redirecting every false shame she has carried, helping her to understand where the shame came from, and where it belongs. *I* get to be the one to let her be messy; *I* am able to let her be silly and enjoy her silliness; *I* can be a safe place for her to share her tears and her sadness, and I will cry with her and grieve with her. *I* will be the one to sit with her in her loneliness; *I* will help her put words to her fears; *I* will show her gentleness, kindness, and patience; *I* will be the one who sees her and speaks the truth over her. *I* will pray and petition God on her behalf, seeking out His truth and His heart for her, and I will share with her how He sees her and loves her. And *I* will be the one to simply ask her how she is, and listen to the answer.

As I have gone through this process, I have explored and expressed much of the above through writing. Knowing where to begin can be a challenge. Yet for me, this was a key part of the process. Making the time and effort to pursue my heart in writing, however difficult it might be, is *giving my heart a voice.*

If writing feels like a daunting task or if you struggle to know where to begin, take heart. There are so many ways to actively pursue our healing through writing. We don't have to be facing a tragic loss or an overload of emotions to begin pursuing our hearts. Below I will share several suggestions for how to begin exploring and pursuing our hearts through writing. I recommend taking one suggestion at a time (in no particular order) and for as long as needed, writing about it whether it takes an hour, a few days or weeks, or for some suggestions, coming back to them as often as needed (as you would with set-ups, for example). My prayer is that these will not feel like tasks to be completed; instead, I pray there will be many aspects of this process that bring comfort and joy; that the healing you will gain as you experience revelation and increased self-awareness through this process will open up new doors and pathways in your life, and will give you fresh hope and a new freedom to be your most authentic, real self; and that even the hard parts, like discovering your own imperfections and grieving the past, will bring release that ushers in peace, genuine humility, and a new perspective on your life and relationships.

Here are just some of the ways we can begin to give a voice to that little boy or little girl of our childhood, who is the picture of our true heart:

Meeting and Getting to Know Myself as a Child
Take some time to think about your childhood, and write about the memories that seem to stand out. Write about all kinds of memories: happy memories, sad memories, fun memories, warm memories, times that you felt afraid, lonely, loved, seen or unseen, etc. Find pictures of yourself as a child to look at as you think about your childhood. Write about yourself as a child, describing your appearance, your likes and dislikes, a special toy, blanket, or books you remember. Write about adults, siblings, or friends that you trusted, admired, or felt close to, as well as anyone you mistrusted or by whom you felt overlooked, disrespected, or mistreated. While looking at your childhood pictures, write about how you feel about the child in the pictures.

When I think of my childhood, I think of the big white house with black trim. Some of my favorite memories of life in this place are: walking up the block to the little church where my dad preached and my mom played the piano every Sunday morning; playing Dukes of Hazard in the backyard with my brother and my friend who lived across the street; making stained glass Christmas ornaments and drinking Russian Tea; my Strawberry Shortcake lunchbox packed with love by Mom and a matching thermos full of milk; peering into a big, cardboard box full of pudgy, pink husky puppies after our dog, Cana had her babies; driving to the dump with my dad because he would let us sit on his lap and steer the truck; wooly, pink footy-pajamas; being tucked in with hugs and kisses and a little song; waking up in the morning to the smell of bacon, and making my sleepy way to our crackling, wood-burning stove, where it was always warm and toasty. I treasure these sweet memories. But there are some painful memories too: having my horse stolen, being overlooked and feeling left out, and the painful circumstances that I experienced because of my parents' divorce.

Pursuing My Little Boy or Girl

Ask yourself, as that little boy or little girl, questions, and then write the answer from his or her perspective. Questions like: How are you feeling today? What do you need from me? Do you feel seen by me? Why or why not? What are you feeling nervous about? Why do you feel sad tonight? What do you think of this situation?

When I do this exercise, it helps if I can picture myself as a little girl, or look at childhood pictures, and then imagine her talking to me (the adult me). What would she say to me?

Letting My Little Boy or Girl Be a Child

For many years, I would come away from a situation or a conversation and feel ashamed or embarrassed at myself for something I said or did. After I began to see my heart as the little girl of my childhood, my focus shifted from blaming and shaming her, to forgiving, accepting, and even embracing her in these moments. If you have experienced this, it may be that a part of you is still unhealed, and therefore, still a child in that area. Your heart—that little boy or little girl—needs to know that you accept them, love them, and treasure them, no matter what—even if they said or did something silly. It's OK. The truth is, in the unhealed places, we are all still that little boy or little girl.

Accepting All the Parts—Even the Messy Parts

It is important to come to a place of acknowledgement and acceptance of where you are right now. Ask yourself: *Can I admit and even make peace with the fact that I am a bit of a mess right now?* This in itself can take time. Who doesn't want to be the one who has it together, who has all the answers? We want to be seen as being strong and capable. No one wants to be seen as weak or needy or messy. But in truth, a child *is* weak. A child *is* needy. A child *is* messy. And if in certain areas I am still a child, then in those areas, *I am weak and needy and messy.*

Rather than disapproving or being ashamed or contemptuous toward that part of myself, it is vital to the healing process to be able to embrace every part of me as I am right now—*weakness, neediness, messiness, and all.*

TAKING INVENTORY

Make lists—of life dreams, longings, disappointments, and fears. These are just to name a few. Give yourself time to sit, think, or pray about what other kinds of lists might provide some helpful insight for you. As I was processing through writing during my most intensive healing months, I spent time writing about relationships I had experienced as an adult, dating relationships as well as friendships, taking note of what unhealthy systems and dynamics may have been at work within those relationships. I wrote about specific men in my life and how I had betrayed my own heart as I searched for love and acceptance through relationships.

Taking inventory helps us to recognize patterns in the survival systems we have utilized, the kinds of relationships we have chosen, and the ways we have operated. This can help us in seeing and processing other aspects of our hearts, such as deeper longings we have had, underlying motives for our actions, etc. It gives us the opportunity to see ourselves and other people a bit more objectively. For me, it stirred up anger at the injustice of how much life had been stolen because of the unhealed wounds and lies that resided within me. It gave me not only motivation to fight for my own heart, but a passion and desire to fight for the hearts of others as well.

EXPLORING SET-UPS

Set-ups are a good way to begin to recognize original wounds and false Heart Beliefs. Begin writing about a set-up by describing the situation. Then, go through and answer the questions from "Questions to Ask with a Set-up" at the end of chapter ten, as many as you feel led to answer. If you have trouble identifying your emotions, use the Emotions List in APPENDIX B to help you put your finger on what it was you were feeling in the situation.

If you are still having trouble identifying your emotions regarding the situation/set-up, take some time to pray and ask for revelation of the truth about what is going on inside. And try asking your heart—your little girl, or little boy—how they felt in those moments. Think of a child standing next to you in the situation, holding your hand, silently pleading for you to stand up for them—to choose them, protect them, and speak up for them. This is, in a way, what is happening in the moment of this present-day situation (set-up). Now, how did you handle it? Did you betray that child in some way, out of a fear of displeasing another person? Did you get angry with him, speaking harsh words to him inside? Did you abandon her? Did she feel unseen, silenced, or disregarded? Did you shame or blame that child or take on any shame (putting it on your little boy or girl) that wasn't yours to take on?

If you are still struggling to identify emotions specifically, try sharing the situation with your trusted friend, mentor, or counselor, and ask for their input about it.

ACKNOWLEDGEMENT OF
WRONGS AND ANGER AT INJUSTICE

As you are able to identify the emotions evoked through a set-up, it is important to trace the emotion back to when you originally experienced it. What was the original wound that caused you to feel this emotion? Now is our chance as we revisit these original wounds, to get angry at the injustice against our hearts and all that has been stolen! Remember that the lens gets twisted because no one acknowledged the injustice against my heart as a child. Now is my chance to right that wrong—I can be the one to acknowledge the wrongs against her. As I acknowledge the injustice toward my own heart, seeing that it happened to this little girl I am getting to know and love, something begins to change. When I acknowledge that she was wronged, and that she did not deserve to be wronged, I am validating her worth, calling her worthy to be treated with kindness and respect, and worthy to be loved. I am acknowledging her intrinsic value, and this is so important for her to know and believe. With this acknowledgement, I am lifting off the false shame that she has carried. Until this happens, she cannot rest or be at peace. Until she is at rest, I will continue to feel her unrest and all that lies underneath it, including her feelings of worthlessness, insecurity, and shame. I am the one she waits for. I am the one she needs.

MAKING TIME AND SPACE TO GRIEVE

As I am able to explore set-ups by identifying the emotions being evoked, tracing them back to original wounds, and acknowledging the injustice against myself as a little girl, there are often many new emotions mixed with the old that come with this process. Revisiting an original wound, we are allowing ourselves to revisit the original emotions that accompanied that incident. This could mean experiencing anew feelings of rejection, betrayal, abandonment, anxiety, panic, powerlessness, fear, vulnerability, humiliation, anger, feeling violated, shame, guilt, self-disgust, or worthlessness. These are some of the common emotions we may experience, but there are many other possibilities as well (see the Negative Emotions list in APPENDIX B).

As we become advocates for our own hearts, we are able to see the injustice from a second point of view as well, which is that of an adult witnessing an injustice against a child, usually by another adult. From this perspective, there is an anger that often rises within us. It is an emotion that a child, who may not fully understand they are being wronged, would not have. There is a righteous anger that should rise as we witness any injustice, but which should especially rise within us on behalf of children. And for me, this anger has not necessarily been directed at my parents or others who sinned against me, but at the robbery that has perpetuated the Great Loss in all of our lives; it is anger at the magnitude of the collective devastation we have experienced simply as inhabitants of a broken, fallen world. It is just as much anger for my parents' losses as for my own. The loss is passed down through generations until someone chooses to draw a line in the sand, so to speak, and fight for the hearts. Pursuing healing, I am not only fighting for my own heart, but I am also fighting for the hearts of my children and their children, as well as all of my other family members and friends.

Revisiting painful memories, we may experience other emotions as well. Can I see my own little girl in those moments? What emotions are being drawn from deep within me as I witness her pain? Am I able to have a genuine compassion and love for her as I would for any other child? Being able to find a true compassion for this child may take some time, but it is so important in this process. As we find this compassion and grieve with our little girl or little boy, the tears we shed on behalf of this child—these are the tears that are unto life because these are the tears that are based in truth, grieving the real injustice against our little girl or little boy (our heart), and which validate the truth of our intrinsic value.

My counselor has said, "to grieve something is to honor it." When we fail to grieve our losses, we are refusing to acknowledge or validate the fact that anything has been lost. In this, we deny what is true, we are not acknowledging reality and dealing with it. We are overlooking the losses we have experienced, and in essence, we are choosing to overlook or ignore the pain experienced by that little girl or little boy of our childhood. When we ignore pain, in the emotional as well as the physical realm, we perpetuate and exacerbate the original problem. Grieving our losses is a necessary part of life and when we refuse to grieve them, we harbor the pain of the losses within, whether or not we know or believe it. We may not 'feel' any pain because we have found ways to cover it, numb it, or escape from it. Yet there it resides, within us.

Another important thing to grieve is our disappointed longings. Burying our longings may be something we have gotten very good at because unfulfilled longings can cause us so much disappointment and pain. But often as we open up our proverbial 'Pandora's Box' of longings in order to begin to listen to our hearts, we may discover that we have, in fact, harbored quite a lot of buried disappointment. We need to give voice to our hearts in this, our longings—to admit that "I had hoped..." and to let the disappointed longing be felt and grieved. If we choose to deaden our hearts and ignore our longings in order to avoid the pain of disappointment, then we also deaden our ability to feel deeply at all, and to fully experience and appreciate all of the good. We miss out on extravagant joy and unexplainable peace, freedom from inhibitions, intimate, heart-to-heart connection with others, and passionate excitement. We miss out on the rich experience that life is meant to be.

FINDING JESUS IN THE PAINFUL PLACES

When my counselor would take me through this process, she would always ask me the same questions: *When did you feel this emotion as a little girl? Can you see her in that moment? How old is she? When you look at her, how do you feel about her?* And then she would always ask, *"Can you see Jesus anywhere?"*

Hebrews 13:5 says "For He Himself has said, 'I will never leave you nor forsake you.'" Jesus experienced first hand the pain of being forsaken on the cross so that we don't ever have to be forsaken. So even in the most painful moments of my childhood, Jesus was present. Somewhere, He was in the room. He was with me. Remembering moments of original wounds, we can ask Him to show us where He was in it.

It is deeply and powerfully healing to process with the Holy Spirit the truth about the past, truths we are freshly admitting to ourselves about what has been lost, and to allow Him to be the One that answers the pain that comes with returning purposely to the memories. Tears unto life come not only from the memory itself, but from once and for all asking with honesty and raw, unbridled emotion "Where were you Lord?" And waiting for the answer—not accusing, but genuinely wanting to know.

The Holy Spirit is the Counselor and He is always willing to reveal as much as we will make time and space for Him to show us. He is the One who gives us understanding of the healing process, and He is the One who ultimately is our Healer. He has created the grieving process in order that we might be able to experience the gift of redemption and healing where there has been pain and loss.

UNDERSTANDING MY OWN LONELINESS

One of the biggest challenges for me during this process was facing loneliness. Because the time of my healing was a season of isolation in a way, there were many days and nights that I felt great loneliness and was tempted to alleviate it in many ways that would have only hindered my healing; it would have been covering, escaping, or numbing the pain, which of course would perpetuate the problem. The truth was, when I was experiencing loneliness, I was really feeling the loneliness of *the little girl* that is my heart. And what's more, it was not only a feeling of loneliness, but there was a terror that would come with it. I would literally feel terror at the thought of being alone for the rest of my life. But as I began to choose to sit still and be in it—to face it and just let myself feel the loneliness rather than running from it, I was actually making space to be able to receive revelation of the truth. This is when I began to see that it was the loneliness of my little girl—my heart—that I was experiencing. For years I did not know her, did not see her, and did not want to be alone with her (with myself). I would constantly abandon her, leaving her in order to pursue friends and social engagements, chasing after the acceptance and approval of others, attempting to fill voids and escape from myself. I worked hard to keep myself occupied—so that I would not feel the loneliness. But in doing this, I was leaving *her* alone. So she felt lonely. So *I* felt lonely. At the end of every day, I felt lonely.

When I began to face my loneliness, I began to see my own heart. I finally had eyes to see my little girl, and I began to actually want to spend time with her! And the more I was able to spend time with my own heart and allow myself to feel whatever emotions were coming in those times, much of the loneliness dissipated. After that, most of the time, I was at peace with the solitude and actually enjoyed my own company. I still have days when I feel lonely, as I think everyone does, but I can allow it to be a signal to me to pause and take note. Loneliness can be a good thing—rather than being something to escape, it is a gift, letting me know I need to take some time to listen to my heart.

SEEKING GOD'S HEART ON BEHALF OF MY CHILD

At times when I would feel especially discouraged, alone, dull, or just didn't know what to believe anymore, I would begin to pray and ask God to show me His heart toward me. Then I would wait and listen. What would God say about me right now? What would He say about my heart? What would He have said to me as a little girl? I would begin to write to my little girl, telling her how God feels about her, speaking truth over her about how loved and how valuable she is to God and to me. Sometimes I would write from God's perspective, as though I were writing a letter from God to myself. Here is an excerpt from one of my prayer sessions:

JULY 2012

My beautiful one, you are my reflection to a brokenhearted world. You are experiencing their pain [within your own] and you are being led by my hand through your healing. This is to bring life out of the seeds that have fallen to the ground and died. Life springing up from the ground. Your tears water the ground and bring life, give birth to new beauty and truth seen through new eyes, restored sight, redeemed heart. That's where the truth is coming through, filtered through the love and compassion and wisdom and new wine I have been pouring into, stirring, and cultivating inside of you during this season of solitude and healing. Never despise your pain. Be thankful for your pain, for it tells you the truth, it warns you of the problems and wounds that still need healing. Your pain is a gift that is going to birth /produce a new harvest of healing. Your life is a living sacrifice, pleasing and acceptable to me. I am pleased with you; I am for you and not against you. I have love and life to fill you up with, and will not disappoint you. Believe my words, my truth about your life, the truth about Who I am, my goodness, my loving-kindness, my righteousness and justice, my love for the world. Believe that there is a bigger picture than what you can see.

MY LIFE—MY RESPONSIBILITY

The ones who wounded us or failed to see our hearts, wronged us; but it is we, ourselves, who have responded in ways that perpetuate the pain and brokenness of our own hearts, and we carry this brokenness into our relationships, sinning against others because of it as well. This process is not about blaming our parents or anyone else.

Rather, it is about becoming an advocate for my own heart, bringing the truth out into the light, recognizing false shame and where it belongs, if not to me, and speaking up for that little girl or boy who may not have even understood that they were being wronged.

As an adult, it is my responsibility to pursue the best life I can. When my brokenness is revealed to me, I am the only one who is able—even responsible before God—to pursue healing in whatever ways I can, because my choice to remain and live out of my unhealed wounds and my twisted lens reaches much farther than I can ever imagine. My choice to remain comfortable in my survival systems affects not only myself, but runs over into all of my relationships. It also reaches through my relationships into the lives of all who are in relationship with those in my circle. And it reaches down through generations affecting my children, their children, and all of the generations that follow.

What is inside of me flows out—whatever that is; whether it is life, light and truth, or a twisted version of reality, as seen from within the walls of my brokenness. I fail to see the hearts of others if I cannot see my own. I fail to connect deeply with others if I operate in systems of self-protection. I fail to pursue the hearts of those I love when I am too busy avoiding my own through systems of escape, busyness, addiction, or self-medication. I fail to share my authentic self with others when I hide using systems of pride, false positivism, spiritualizing, people-pleasing, saying what others want to hear, perfectionism, superiority, or contempt (of self or others) through humor, sarcasm, or disrespect. I hurt others when the unhealed parts of me are 'provoked' and I react, whether through active or passive aggression. I may shut others out, punish, act disrespectfully or with disdain, avoid them, or write them off altogether. I may use words or attitudes of contempt, blame, shaming, domination or intimidation, criticism, judgment, negativism, argumentativeness, or a religious spirit.

It is with desperation that I have prayed—*Lord, I don't want to do this to the people I love (especially my children!) Do whatever it takes to change me!* I believe we all have the desire to love others well, and part of this is taking responsibility for our own hearts and our emotional health. The good news is that healing and change are always available, if we are open and ready to pursue the truth.

QUESTIONS TO CONSIDER

Take a few minutes to look at one or a few childhood pictures. How do you feel about the child in the pictures? How does it make you feel to think of becoming an advocate for him/her?

Can you identify one or more wounds/losses in your life that you have not acknowledged or been able to grieve? If so, can you think of anything that may be hindering you from letting yourself begin to process the loss?

Nearly everyone struggles with loneliness to some degree or another. If you struggle with loneliness, spend some time writing about how you have responded to feelings of loneliness. If you have generally tried to 'get away' from this emotion when it comes, what has that looked like? What if next time you experience feelings of loneliness, you were to purposely 'look it in the eye,' so to speak? (For example, to sit and just be in the loneliness, without trying to get away from it; pray and ask for revelation of where it is coming from, and anything else that would bring truth to light regarding your loneliness.)

Love takes off the masks that we fear we cannot live without and know we cannot live within. I use the word "love" here not merely in the personal sense but as a state of being, or a state of grace—not in the infantile American sense of being made happy but in the tough and universal sense of quest and daring and growth.

JAMES BALDWIN

THE FIRE NEXT TIME

CHAPTER 13

More About the Process

FOR MANY, THE PROSPECT OF FACING THE PAST AND re-experiencing painful emotions is daunting, or downright terrifying. This is understandable. It is no small thing to choose to pursue our hearts through this healing process. It requires great courage.

It is true that there will be tears and there will be painful memories, but when tears are unto life, they bring healing, and relief. In our tears, we are grieving not only the hurt from the wound itself, but all that has been lost as a result of the wound and the false messages that came with it. The relief comes because we are finally recognizing these messages. We are stepping out of agreement with them, we are seeing the truth, and we are choosing to invite the truth in to replace the lie we believed. With truth comes freedom. "And you shall know the truth, and the truth shall make you free," (John 8:32).

Not only does healing bring freedom, it produces a peace that cannot be experienced any other way. This is a peace that comes when lies are replaced with truth, and when wrongs from the past are made right within us. Healing also changes the dynamic in our relationships, retraining us to implement healthy boundaries within our existing relationships, and naturally drawing us to emotionally healthy people more and more as we continue to heal. My new boundaries may stir things up for someone else, but that may be an important part of their journey.

When we finally turn to face what we have long avoided, we are choosing to take responsibility for ourselves, and when we take responsibility for ourselves, it means we have a say in what happens next. As you choose to embrace whatever it is God wants to do in your heart and your life, this may be the question that comes up: *What happens next?* When you have said 'Yes' to the healing journey, it doesn't usually take very long before the set-ups start happening. However, if you feel like you are waiting for some answers and want to purposefully set out in pursuit of your heart, there are some things you can do.

ASKING THE RIGHT QUESTIONS

One of the most valuable things I did as I went through this process was to ask questions. I would pray and ask for direction and revelation, then I would wait, then questions would come, and I would write them down, and then I would answer them. I discovered many things in this way that I had not, and probably would not have considered otherwise.

Why Questions

Why questions are good because they give us insights into our motivations, our longings and desires, and our fears. They also usually lead to other kinds of questions that dig deeper into the truth of what lies underneath, what it is that's compelling us to do what we do. *Why* do I spend so much time on social media? (What am I looking for? What is the *need* or *longing* I am trying to fill?) *Why* am I working so hard to please this person and keep them happy? (What am I *afraid* will happen if I disappoint them or tell them 'no'? What is the *fear?*) *Why* do I _____ (clean compulsively, shut down with my spouse, lose my temper with my kids, escape by turning to food, alcohol, sex, social media, television, work, etc.) Granted, the answer to this one may not necessarily be obvious or simple, but it is a necessary first question, a catalyst to get us to the deeper questions and answers.

What Questions

We can get creative with *What* questions—the possibilities are endless. *What* questions are great for digging deeper, exploring, and discovering. Often, in this process, I would pray and ask God to show me something I couldn't quite put my finger on—an emotion, a motive, an unexplained feeling of shame or sadness or anxiety. I might simply ask *What is this God?* His answer would often come by way of another *What* question. I have learned so much about myself I had not known because I began to ask *What?*

    What do I think will happen if...? *What* is stopping me from...? *What* is the fear attached to...? *What* does it say about me if I fail at...? *What* do I need from...? *What* are my longings and desires? *What* is the disappointed longing—*what* had I hoped for? *What* would I choose if I weren't afraid of...? And one of my favorite questions as I sought to know my own heart—Heart, (addressing myself as a little girl), *what* do you think about this situation? *What* do you see?

When Questions

When questions are important because they help us to think about the true origin of an emotion. It is often stemming from something in the past, more so than from the immediate situation. The answer usually leads us to the memory of a wound that needs to be addressed. If we can start to recognize when our buttons are being pushed—start to notice what kinds of things cause us to shut us down or to get fired up—then we can work on identifying the specific emotion(s) that are coming up in these moments. Once we can do this, then we can ask *When*? *When* have I felt this way before? Was there a specific time that I felt this way as a child? A teenager? A young adult? (First identify the emotion, then ask, *When...*)

Who Questions

The main *Who* question that comes to mind is: God, *Who* do You say I am? *Who* am I according to Your Word? And another important question is, *Who* is this little boy or little girl in my childhood pictures?

Where Questions

Where are these fears coming from? *Where* am I presently, in terms of mental and emotional readiness to ask all of the hard questions? Am I all in? Or is it more than I want, or have time, or energy, or even just the heart to look at right now? And the enjoyable, dreaming questions like, *Where* do I want to be in 5 or 10 years? *Where* would I go if I could go anywhere without restriction of time or finances?

LOOKING FOR LOVE, LIFE, WORTH FROM THE EXTERNALS

When we do begin to ask these questions, we often find that we are looking to tangible, external places and things, to find the intangible. The longing to feel loved. The need to feel like my life has significance. The desire to be seen.

We may discover we have desperately needed the approval of others in order to 'feel good about myself' or to 'be OK.' We may discover that much of what we do is performance-based or success-driven because somewhere underneath, we believe that we must perform or be successful in order to be of any worth or value to anyone (or to have any worth or value at all). We may realize that we are avoiding life and the truth of our inward condition, and choosing instead to cope through escapes, addictions, or even just staying busy all the time.

THE FRUIT OF UNHEALED WOUNDS

There are so many different ways that our wounds and false beliefs affect our inner condition. We may live with a shame-based identity, which can look like many things on the outside such as pride, performance, blame, contempt, etc. We may find that we struggle again and again with feelings of rejection or wanting to belong (feeling left out). We may find it challenging to trust people or God because we have experienced deep feelings of abandonment or betrayal in the past. We may discover that we have not been living with healthy, appropriate boundaries in our relationships.

In this process, there arise what I will call BIG words—words that are capitalized and loaded with meaning and complexity. Some of the BIG words I came up against throughout my own healing process were:

Shame
Self-hatred
Judgment of Self/Others
Rejection
Abandonment
Betrayal
Codependency
Boundaries
Perfectionism

I have included a list of resources that address several of the above topics specifically and in depth, many of which have significantly impacted me throughout this process (See APPENDIX C for this list of resources). If you are working through your healing process with a counselor or mentor, they will be able to help you identify and navigate through whatever BIG words come up for you as you begin to purposely face and address wounds and losses from the past.

I want to mention briefly one concept in particular that was especially revelatory for me as I was working through my own struggle with rejection.

Elijah House Ministries is an inner-healing ministry founded by John and Paula Sanford. There is a free audio teaching on their website under the 'Resource' page entitled "Understanding Bitter Roots." It is a teaching based on a verse in Hebrews that says, "See to it that no one fails to obtain the grace of God; that no 'root of bitterness' springs up and causes trouble, and by it many become defiled," (Hebrews 12:15 ESV). In this teaching, Sanford teaches about what he calls 'bitter root judgments' and 'bitter root expectancies.'

The basic concept is that when we are sinned against as a child (whether by sin of commission or omission), a bitter root springs up within us that causes us to make a judgment against and/or to have an expectancy of that behavior from others. When this happens, we carry this judgment or expectancy with us into adulthood, and we unintentionally and unknowingly draw this behavior to ourselves from others again and again. "For with the judgment you pronounce, you will be judged, and with the measure you use, it will be measured to you," (Matthew 7:2 ESV).

A 'bitter root judgment' is our sinful response to being sinned against. It is based on a spiritual law and as such, it will continue to operate within us until we are brought to the revelation of it and choose to address it. Unless this happens, it will continue to affect us, and those around us, defiling them also. 'Defiling others' means that my bitter root has the power to draw out a certain kind of response or behavior from another person. Sanford gives the example in his teaching that you may sit down next to someone and spend some time with that person, and walk away feeling good; yet you can sit with someone else and after awhile, feel unclean. That person may have a bitter root that has 'defiled' you.

When we recognize that we are harboring a bitter root judgment or expectancy, then we are able to forgive, repent, confess, and bring our judgment to the cross, putting it to death once and for all so that we can be forgiven and have freedom in that area.

As I have shared, I struggled a great deal with feelings of rejection. After hearing this teaching, I began to see how my own bitter root of rejection had drawn this experience of feeling rejected by others to myself again and again. It was such a huge relief to get some kind of answer to this, even though it was hard to hear that the problem was actually within myself. It is a comfort zone to blame others for the pain that we repeatedly feel, but since the only person I can change is myself, it is in reality such a good gift to know that I can do something about the problem. Even still, it is God who, through the cross of Jesus, puts to death the bitter roots within us, bringing us into a new freedom.

On the same 'Resource' page, there is another very good teaching called "Hearts of Stone and Inner Vows." I highly recommend listening to both the "Bitter Roots" and the "Hearts of Stone" audios, as they are both extremely insightful, and were for me a great revelation of the spiritual principles that had been operating in my life. It is also helpful as an insight into what may be happening in others as well.

QUESTIONS TO CONSIDER

Do you believe that the pain of facing the past is worth it? Is the desire to live healed and free from the strongholds of the past GREATER than the fear or dread of revisiting painful memories? Journal about your answer, whether you answered yes or no.

Write down two or three questions each of Why questions, What questions, When questions, Who questions, and Where questions. They can be about your childhood, the past, the present or the future. After you have finished coming up with questions, take some time to thoroughly answer at least one question from each category.

Are there any ways that you can think of in which you have been looking for life, love, or worth from the Externals? If so, write down your thoughts about it.

PART IV

Living Healed

I don't want to be little again. But at the same time I do. I want to be me like I was then, and me as I am now, and me like I'll be in the future. I want to be me and nothing but me. I want to be crazy as the moon, wild as the wind and still as the earth. I want to be every single thing it's possible to be.

DAVID ALMOND

JACKDAW SUMMER

CHAPTER 14

Integration

AS WE HEAL, WE ARE RECOVERING BITS AND PIECES OF ourselves back from all of the times we have left behind, betrayed, or rejected our own hearts, which we have done again and again. In the process of pursuing healing, we are pulling the child out of that cycle and now instead, we become their safe place. Now we are getting reacquainted with that little girl or little boy who had been left behind and has waited all this time to be seen. We are learning what she likes and doesn't like. We are finding out how she feels about the situations we experience. We are enquiring of his wants. We are prioritizing his needs. We begin to consider the opinions, preferences, and perspective of that child as we go through our days making decisions, as we interact with others, and as we face challenges and conflicts.

Taking on my little girl's perspective, everything looks different. She is drawn to different kinds of people than I was. She is drawn to safe people, to people that see her and want to know her. She has no interest in spending time with people who are disregarding of or contemptuous toward her. Getting to know my heart as a child is very useful in gauging the kind of company I keep. Checking in with how she is feeling around certain people is kind of like observing how someone treats the waiter—it tells me everything I need to know. I so appreciate the Maya Angelou quote that says, "When someone shows you who they are, believe them." And yet, through the twisted lens, I often could not recognize that there was anything wrong when others, operating in unhealthy systems, were actually disregarding or disrespecting my heart (and/or their own).

Now though, as I am getting to know this little girl, I am 'seeing' with increasing discernment, and with clarity. She sees more than I ever did apart from her. She feels it when someone is 'pulling' on her. She recognizes when someone's 'generosity' may be unknowingly driven by mixed motivations. She can usually recognize the masks that others are wearing. She also sees the hearts (the little girls and boys) of other people, even when they are being critical, controlling, contemptuous, etc. Even now, when I am disconnected from her, I miss it. But if I can take some time with her, I regain clarity and am able to see 'behind the scenes' again.

Getting to know her preferences, I am getting to know my own. I used to live a bit oblivious to my likes and dislikes. For example, after years of eating raw mushrooms in my mom's salads, I took the time one day in the middle of eating another one of her (otherwise yummy) salads to consider that I don't actually like raw mushrooms. In fact, I have always really, really disliked them. So why was I eating them? It just never occurred to me to pick them out and not eat them. Thank You, Lord— I have been set free from raw mushrooms! It's a silly example, but at the same time, it's a big deal. The important thing to ask is, *why* do we do the things we do? And here is the big deal: Why? Because I developed a pattern of ignoring, to the point of becoming numb to my own preferences, in order to please people—I never wanted to rock the boat.

I remember being about 5 years old and pretending to like Brussels sprouts when really, I hated them. My brother hated them and he would complain about having to eat them. I wanted to be seen as good and to make my parents happy with me, so much so that I choked them down with as much enthusiasm on my face as I could muster. I wanted to make sure they knew that I was the one who was not giving them any grief about my Brussels sprouts. Yes, I ate my veggies, but I wasn't being honest or true to myself. Living this way for so many years, I was living numb to myself, not knowing myself. Beginning to heal gave me this part of myself back.

Consequently, not knowing what I liked or disliked contributed to having difficulty with decision-making. Of course, I just thought of myself as indecisive. But as I began to get to know myself, I also began to be able to make decisions more quickly and easily.

It has been a joy to become a mom for the same reason. I am continuing to learn more about myself, almost daily. Yesterday I was sitting at a little table with my almost 3-year-old daughter, making crafts. Before I was a mom, the thought of doing crafts made me go "Ewww." But here I was, and you know what? I was loving it! I mean really enjoying it, and really getting into it, probably even more than she was. What a gift it is, to be able to share this simple pleasure with my sweet daughter, my heart overflowing, and my own inner child thoroughly delighting in the process of creating lots of beautiful things imperfectly—just for the joy of it. Another little piece of me is back.

And this is what it looks like to collect the pieces of myself back together from where I left them behind. The fruit that comes from this healing journey is manifold and bountiful, layered and inter-connected, and often unexpected. As we heal, we are being given back what was taken away. Even something as simple as knowing my own tastes is incredibly important to take back because it is a piece, however small, of the honest truth about who I am. If I do not know who I am, how then can I offer anything to others that is authentic—that is from the Real Me and truly from the heart? I can't. Neither can I experience true heart connection and intimacy with others if I do not know my own heart. True self-awareness is really heart-awareness, and heart-awareness is what allows me to pursue and love others from my heart.

In getting to know who I am, there is an integration that is taking place—who I really am (at my core, my true heart) is being deposited, piece by piece, back into the 'me' that people see and encounter. The Real Me—who I was created to be—is being restored and revived. I am being reunited with my own heart!

It is important to acknowledge that this process of healing is not something I am able to do by my own strength or power of thought or reason. The healing that we are experiencing through this process is only made possible by the death and resurrection of Jesus because through His sacrifice, death was defeated. Not just His own physical death—all Death. The claim Death would have on all of creation as a result of the fall and the entrance of sin into our collective picture—this has been nullified. And though the law of sin is still at work in us, as Paul talks about in Romans 7, we now have access not only to eternal life—the invitation to live forever with Jesus—but we have been given the power of Life (over Death) in the here and now.

So even though Death seemed to have its say in my life when original wounds and their false messages robbed me of the life I was created for, redemption comes through the healing power of Jesus. *And redemption restores with a bigger and better return than anything that was ever taken away.*

As the 'grown-up' me is being reunited with the delightful little girl that is my heart, Life is literally being poured into me like water. When this happens, I will begin to see and experience that this Life is flowing out of me and into the lives and hearts of others.

Whether or not we are truly offering Life to others depends on the place from which all of our actions and words flow. What is the deepest motivation for what I do and say? Are my actions coming from a need to perform or to impress someone or feel worthy of their praise? Or are my actions flowing out of my heart, because that thing brings me life? Are my words flowing out of a need to please someone and gain their approval? Or from a heart that simply desires to encourage them, and to give without expecting any returns? Whatever motivates me is going to flow out of me, whether I want it to or not. When I am *giving* or *doing* in order to *get* (validation, acceptance, love, etc.), it can feel to others like I am taking or trying to pull from them (even if they don't really understand why). When just *being me* is enough, then I will become a vessel out of which Life can flow to others.

QUESTIONS TO CONSIDER

Think about a recent situation or interaction from which you came away feeling bad, though you may not have been able to put your finger on what it was. Now imagine yourself as a little boy or little girl, being the one in that situation, and that the other person/people involved were talking to you. Ask the child: How did you feel being with that person? What was said or done that made you feel bad? Did I say or do anything that made you feel bad? In writing, answer these questions as though from the perspective of your little boy or little girl, as if they are sharing how they felt with you.

Do you ever feel indecisive? Do you sometimes find it hard to know what you want or need? If so, next time you are faced with a decision, try this: Close your eyes and picture yourself as a little boy or little girl. Then ask that child what he/she needs or wants you to choose.

As you are becoming more aware of your own survival systems, when faced with decisions, begin to ask yourself: Is this action or decision rooted in performance or needing someone's approval, or am I choosing this because it truly brings me life?

The opposite of love is not hate. The opposite of love is self-protection.

PAT STARK

THE STORY OF LIFE

CHAPTER 15

A New Way

LIVING FROM MY HEART

IN LISTENING TO THE VOICE OF THAT LITTLE GIRL AND living in a way that considers her, cares for her, and prefers her, integration is continually taking place. As this happens, and I am being reunited with my own heart, **I begin to actually live my life** *from my heart* **rather than living out of a mask, separate from my heart.** My innermost being, who I am at my core, gets to have a say and participates with me again as I interact with the world around me and as I make decisions. With hardly any effort, I naturally begin to make decisions based more on my own needs and preferences rather than on what others may expect or want from me. I no longer feel the need to please or impress others in order to gain their approval—I simply approve of myself. I begin to feel valuable and loved, and I begin to feel comfortable in my own skin. **I am the only one that has to approve of me and it doesn't matter what others say or believe about me.** This is liberating and truly empowering! It allows me to bring myself to the table and say without apologizing: *Here I am—the Real Me. Whatever you think* *is OK because my identity is not contingent upon whether or not you accept, approve of, or affirm me.* This comes from a place of rest and confidence, free of any need or expectation of another person. And this is refreshing for others to encounter because it does not require them to prop me up, tell me I'm OK, excuse me, approve of me, etc.

Some may see these words and think—*I have always been that way*—*"Here I am: take it or leave it!"* Yet the heart behind those words can often be more of a defiant or proud attitude. *That* is not *this*. In this, I come to the table with a generosity of spirit, not daring others to disapprove, not assuming they will judge me. Rather, I assume nothing, and I simply invite them to experience ME.

Living from my heart, my lens becomes one of Love. Where once my perceptions were colored and even dictated by things like self-protection, fear, control, or shame, now Love becomes the lens. When I see through a lens of Love, I assume the best. I trust. I live generously. I freely give and receive (gifts—tangible and intangible, words of praise or encouragement, approval). I am not easily offended. I allow myself to cry, to make mistakes, to be messy. I take each day and each encounter as it comes without worrying or trying to control how it goes, and without being attached to any outcome. I let go of my pictures, allowing the blank canvas of the unknown to exist before me without fear or specific expectation, in peace. And I am OK, however things go.

Living from my heart I settle into a new *modus operandi*. Living from my heart I am choosing to live and love by way of...

VULNERABILITY VS. SELF-PROTECTION

I now have eyes to see my own heart and I am learning to understand these truths about her: she is intrinsically valuable, she is worthy of love and respect, and she is good. With this new understanding, I gain two things: first, I gain the ability to be transparent, which comes with getting free from the need to hide my heart from others—there is no shame or fear attached to the thought of someone really knowing me; second, because I do not need the approval of others, I am able to be myself and to come from a place of love as I relate to others, which naturally translates as giving—rather than taking, pulling on, or needing something from them.

What does this look like? Love comes bearing gifts. It comes offering itself without agenda and without expecting returns. Love is not 'cool' and has no need to impress or prove anything to anyone. Love doesn't people-please—it respects others enough to be honest, and to say no—not always yes. Love doesn't pull on people. It isn't searching for anything from others, it just brings itself to the table. And Love doesn't stand people up (in the literal or figurative sense)—it shows up, letting itself be seen and experienced by others.

Coming to the table with transparency and with Love means I am no longer operating in a 'self-protect' mode. Our systems of self-protection develop because we have felt unsafe or exposed, or have experienced pain as a result of our vulnerability. But self-protection keeps us isolated and disconnected from the hearts of others. Living this way, not only do our own hearts miss out, but being focused on staying safe, we disregard the hearts of others. What we might have to offer them is ungiven.

Self-protection can show up in many forms. For some, a guarded, cynical, or contemptuous approach gets the job done just fine. But for those of us who are more socially inclined, there are subtler ways to self-protect. For example, self-protection might look like generosity when someone always insists on picking up the check, but refuses reciprocity. It can be at work in the friend who is always the one with the answers, always the one to counsel, advise, teach, and encourage—but is never on the receiving end. Self-protection is certainly a part of many of the survival systems we use to hide our hearts. It can look like: niceness or sweetness, intelligence, efficiency/competence, criticism or judgment, avoidance, measured words/over thinking, not trying for fear of failure, and more.

As we take the time to face the past, many of the false messages that have kept us bound up and committed to our self-protection are replaced with the truth. The false messages convinced us that others would betray us. They have made us feel unsafe and have kept us on high alert, never able to rest or fully trust anyone. When our wounds are healed and these messages are replaced with the truth, then we are released from our hyper-vigilance and are able to be at rest in understanding that: Yes, life can (and will) at times be painful, and yes, it will still be possible for others to hurt or betray me. *Yet I am safe in the absolute and perfect love of God. He accepts me and I accept me.*

Knowing that I am loved and approved of by God and by myself, there is no longer a need for me to fear the words or actions of others. Allowing myself the risk of vulnerability, I am making room in my life for the opportunity to experience true connection and intimacy with others, deep joy, and an abiding rest within.

TRUST VS. CONTROL

This unpredictable thing called Life, in all of its perpetual messiness, pain, and beauty, has a way of letting us know that we are absolutely *not* in control. As my counselor often says, life is full of mixture, and full of gifts and losses. We are not promised tomorrow. We are not promised our pictures or our dreams. We are not promised anything—or at least any earthly thing. We cannot see what lies ahead, and for some, this feels overwhelming and can bring up feelings of fear or anxiety. This is where many struggle with the need to create some kind of security for themselves through control.

But being 'in control' is an illusion. Although we know that it is not possible to know the future, or to control circumstances, events, or other people, our unhealed wounds and our fears *compel* us to try anyway. We may try to control by means of domination, manipulation, guilt, shaming, perfectionism, compulsive or obsessive behaviors, collecting knowledge, withholding love to punish, micromanaging, overachieving, underachieving, getting our ducks in a row, and more. And at the end of the day, the fact remains—*we are not in control!* And we are not meant to be.

Control is often rooted in fear. Whenever we find ourselves trying to control, we might ask, *What will happen if I let go of trying to control this?* (Some undesirable outcome) *And what if that happens, then what? What am I really afraid of?*

Exploring the answers to some of these questions usually takes us to places in the past where we have felt out of control, overpowered, powerless, or voiceless. Through the healing process, there is a powerful release of the need to create safety and security for ourselves at all costs (control). In fighting for my own heart and becoming her advocate, my heart begins to trust that she is no longer alone, that there is no need to be anxious or to fear, because in becoming her advocate, I am demonstrating a trustworthiness that she can rest in.

For me, as I began to heal, I felt less and less the need to control. As something would come up that was out of my control, instead of trying to figure out how I could make things happen a certain way, I began to look inward. I would evaluate the situation through the lens of what my heart needed. Usually, she just needed *me* to affirm *her*, rather than my trying to get *someone else* to affirm *me*. Once my heart felt secure and fully approved of (by me and by God), I no longer needed things to go any certain way in order to be OK. I could just show up and be myself and let things unfold as they may.

RESPECT AND HONOR VS.
DISRESPECT, SHAME, AND CONTEMPT

Being treated with respect and honor instills within the heart of a child a healthy sense of self-respect. Respect for self is a vital ingredient for a child learning how to develop and maintain healthy, mutually respectful relationships with others.

If I feel my own heart is worthy of disrespect, shame, or contempt, I will want to hide my heart from others. I will wear a mask hoping that others will not discover my true heart. And often, the survival system I use to cover my own shame involves directing shame or contempt toward others.

I want to interject here some thoughts on the importance of treating our children with honor and respect. I believe that to treat a child with respect honors his heart and speaks to the inherent value he possesses as a human and a child of God. Treating him with respect says *I believe your heart is good. I believe that you are worthy of love and respect.* When we treat our children with disrespect, shame, or contempt, not only do we fail to gain the respect from them that we are looking for, but we send them the message that they are not worthy of respect, and so they will come to lack respect for themselves.

It is entirely possible to discipline and teach our children without using disrespect, shame, or contempt. We disrespect our children when, addressing their misbehavior, we attach shame to who they are, rather than helping them develop a healthy sense of right and wrong regarding their behaviors; when we belittle or shame them in front of others, yell at them in frustration or anger, fail to listen, fail to validate their perspective, believe the worst, disregard their emotions, make fun of them or make jokes at their expense (which is really contempt) and call it 'just playing' and more. Yet it is tragically common for parents to treat their children with disrespect simply because they are children, believing it is OK because 'I am the boss' or because this is how they themselves were brought up.

The truth is, our children push our buttons, and what comes out is usually our own 'stuff' and it comes out all over them. Of course, it is impossible to be a perfect parent and we have all made the kinds of mistakes mentioned above. But remember that there is power in acknowledgement. Saying "I'm sorry" and asking for forgiveness goes a long way in keeping a strong, open connection with our kids. Even if our disrespect has been in response to their misbehavior, it is important to acknowledge our wrongdoing. We can apologize for the way we have handled something without condoning their misbehavior. Our children are really just little people who need our love, guidance, and instruction, and who deserve to be treated with respect in order to learn respect for self and others.

Disrespect can look like many things. It might appear as outright disrespect or contempt, but it can also appear as the opposite. For example, if I have a friend who asks for help or favors on a regular basis and I always say yes so as to be that friend that she can always count on, then I may actually be disrespecting this friend, as well as myself. Always saying yes or taking on more than I should can be disrespectful in that when I do this, I am not respecting my friend enough to be honest, because I do not trust that she will be able to handle my honest 'no.' I believe that she will dislike or reject or abandon me if I say 'no,' which is actually assuming the worst about her. So instead, I say yes to keep her happy with me, and forfeit meeting the needs of my own heart in the process. Meanwhile, I am building a growing resentment toward my friend every time I say yes when I should say no.

In this scenario, I not only show my friend disrespect, but I am clearly demonstrating a disrespect for myself in that I am disregarding my own need in order to keep hold of the approval of my friend.

In contrast, as I learn to love and respect my own heart, I begin to genuinely love and respect others, and to make decisions that honor my own heart and the hearts of others.

What has this looked like for me? I am learning how to speak up for myself when something feels wrong. I am learning how not to cover over or take upon myself another person's shame. So if they are acting or speaking inappropriately or in a way that makes me feel uncomfortable, I feel free to remove myself from the situation or to say what I think. I no longer believe that I need to protect anyone's ego at the expense of my own heart. I no longer feel responsible for how other people are going to feel or react if I say no to them or disappoint them with my decisions. I am learning to be honest about what I think and how I really feel about things.

RESPONSIBILITY VS. BLAME/PLAYING THE VICTIM

As I begin to heal, I begin to take responsibility for my emotions, my actions, and my decisions. Taking responsibility for myself is about (1) pursuing the truth of my inward condition (this discussion is primarily about emotional health, though taking responsibility certainly includes pursuing spiritual and physical health as well); (2) coming to terms with what is real and what is not (Reality); and (3) embracing the present.

I take responsibility for my life when I choose to pursue the truth of my inward condition and seek healing of the wounds and losses of my past, knowing that unless and until I do, not only do I remain a victim to them, but I allow the bitter fruit of my unhealed wounds to defile those around me, as all that remains inside of me flows out of me and into the lives of those I love.

It takes humility and courage to accept counsel and advice. This is community versus isolation or being 'an island,' and this is the first step to truly taking responsibility for myself. If I am going to be responsible for me, then first things first: *I must be willing to pursue the truth (outside of my own opinion) about what is real and what is not.* Is this possible to do successfully on my own (as an island)? In my opinion, no.

When we are living wounded, we often perceive the words, actions, and 'vibes' of others through our twisted lens. We are not seeing and perceiving things as they really are, but as they make us feel when they touch our wounds. This is why it is so important to seek help from a counselor or a trusted friend—someone who is outside of our situations—to help us consider what 'face value' really is. Then we can hold our own perceptions up to this and ask, *What is it in me then, that feels [hurt, offended, angry]? When have I felt this way in the past?* And so on. In doing this, we may discover that there have been some areas where we have not been accurately interpreting the words and actions of others. This can be humbling, but it is also an encouraging discovery because it usually means a brighter outlook in many of our everyday situations.

As I take responsibility for my life and pursue truth, the wounds that have long skewed my vision begin to be healed, and gradually, the clarity of my vision continues to grows more reliable. I am beginning to perceive things more and more as they really are, so I am less susceptible to being hurt or offended by others. I can now take what I hear at face value and respond accordingly. In fact, I even begin to be able to see the hurting hearts of others underneath negative words and actions, as well as the survival systems that may be at play, so that even when others are acting out of contempt, shame, criticism, judgment, or in other unloving ways, I am still able to respond in love without harboring offense.

I will openly admit that I have not mastered this by any means! I still get hurt, I still get offended more easily than I should, and I still react in unloving ways. But I also have a husband who recognizes when I am probably being set up! He tells me that it's probably a set-up, and I get annoyed, and then I think about it, and then I have a good cry (because he cared enough to tell me the truth), and then we talk about it, and what is underneath? A little hidden, unhealed wound—just waiting there to be noticed.

Responsibility is also about embracing the present. I spent a lot of years in all of the myriad of moments of my life besides the present one. I spent way (way, way) too much time mulling over both failed relationships of yesteryear, and awkward interactions of last week; remembering fallings out that were never resolved, and failures of the past that kept me locked in shame and regret; pining over disappointments that played out in repeating patterns despite how hard I worked to get things to work out the way I wanted them to. The past had such a strong grip on me and it kept me from moving forward in many areas of my life.

And then there was the future. I was tremendously invested in the pictures I had painted for myself of all that hadn't happened yet. I had dreams for my life, but none of them could begin from the present moment. All of my dreams and desires were contingent upon whether or not the pieces of my picture would cooperate and fall into place. And so there was always a reason—an excuse why—I couldn't pursue my dreams and desires...not quite yet.

For many years of my adult life I lived almost exclusively in the past and in the future—never in the present. Not only was I not enjoying my life, I was actually *missing out* on my life. On my healing journey, I felt led to take a long, purposeful look just once more at the collection of small stories that were 'my life' up to that point (I'm referring to the undertaking I mentioned earlier of going through my journals). I knew it would be important for me to be able to process it all through a different lens, and it was a truly redeeming experience. I needed to process the hurts from the past, and then, I needed to let them go.

But there was still more letting go to do. With the help and guidance of my counselor, I was able to identify pictures that I had been clinging to that kept me dwelling on some future point in time. Where did these pictures come from, anyway? What were my true longings and desires? And what about all of the disappointment that I felt as a result of those longings being un-fulfilled? Could I release my disappointed longings to the Lord? Could I let go of my pictures? Could I trust that God is really good? Could I trust that He had my best interest at heart? That He was doing something good in my life right now? Could I take a look at my present and could I choose to embrace my life as it was in that moment—disappointments and all? Coming to terms with reality required wrestling with my present reality—including my disappointments and my questions of God's character and of His heart toward me. These were huge questions for me because getting honest with myself, I felt in many ways that God had forgotten me and that He was not concerned with my heart at all. In fact, I felt abandoned by Him.

Once I had dealt with these and other questions about letting go of past disappointments and future pictures, I could feel myself beginning to be at rest in my present reality. This breakthrough led me quite naturally into a different way of thinking. It birthed in me a new sense of responsibility for my own life, almost as if it were inquiring of me what I might think I'd like to do next? Now that I was free. Now that I knew that my heart (and so also my time) was valuable. Now that I was at liberty to dream up any dream I fan-cied, and now that it did not have to wait for any particular thing to happen first. Now what would I like to do with myself?

In this way of thinking, my thoughts and decisions are not waiting on anyone or any event to propel me to my destiny, and they are not blaming anyone for how my life is going or not going. They are just taking inventory of the present reality, and choosing to fully embrace and experience today—whatever the day will bring. I am still able to rest in the full hope and belief that good things are coming, but I don't have to miss out on my life in the meantime.

HEALTHY BOUNDARIES

Around the time I found myself swimming in some of the deepest waters of my healing journey, I was assigned a book to read as part of a counseling course I was taking. The book was *Boundaries* written by Henry Cloud and John Townsend, and I remembered seeing it as a teenager when I used to frequent the Christian bookstore. Ironically, at that time, I was sure I had no use for it because in my mind I was already pretty much an expert in the area of boundaries. This was, of course, not even close to being true.

I erroneously fancied myself a master at relationships, among other things. In reality, I knew very little about healthy relationships and absolutely nothing about healthy boundaries. I knew co-dependency, I knew walls, I knew reserved suspicion of those who thought too well of me, I knew entrusting myself to the wrong kinds of people, I knew keeping others at a distance, I knew shutting down, and I knew walking away (and occasionally running). I did not know that my closest connections utilized systems of co-dependence, while lacking true intimacy of the heart. And I did not know that I was terrible at saying no. A Boundaries Expert I was not. It was striking how little I knew as I read the book for the first time.

I remember one day in the midst of discovering just how sorely lacking my sense of boundaries was, I got a text from my sister-in-law asking me if I would be able to babysit on what happened to be my next day off. I had already made plans for that day: I was going to spend it at home by myself. I had been looking forward to being able to spend some time writing in order to process some specific things that had happened. I was excited just to be able to enjoy my own company and to not be obligated to anything or anyone else for a whole day.

When the text came in, I wrestled with what to do. I loved spending time with my niece and wanted to be able to help my sister-in-law. As I wrestled, I was realizing that I desperately needed the time for myself, but I also desperately wanted to please my sister-in-law. Finally, knowing now after reading *Boundaries* that it was OK and right for me to say no in this instance, I chose to say no. Sending it, not only did I literally begin to cry, I realized that it was the first time I had said no to her without having any prior obligation to excuse me besides a date with myself. Why was I crying? I had to think about it. I was crying because I was truly afraid—even terrified—that she would get angry with me, and that she might never ask me to babysit again, and I would never get to spend time with my sweet niece again. This was an absurd fear not based in truth. Yet the fear of rejection was a deep, real fear that had for so long compelled me to say yes to people, no matter what—to always put my own heart and my own needs last in order to please people and keep them (so I believed) from rejecting or abandoning me.

I talked earlier about taking responsibility for my own emotions, decisions, and actions. Just as importantly, having healthy boundaries requires that I *do not* take on any false responsibility for the emotions, decisions, and actions of others. This 'responsible for me, not you' dynamic creates freedom within my relationships because I can bring myself to the table—my true heart—without feeling like I need to squeeze myself into a mold that fits your expectation or keeps you happy, and without fear of your reaction to my honesty.

SIMPLE HONESTY VS. EXCUSES AND 'SHOULDS'

As I heal, I begin to trust that my simple honesty is enough. I am learning that I do not owe anyone an explanation or an excuse for my decisions. When I am invited to lunch or asked to do a favor for someone, a simple 'yes' or 'no' is enough. Most of my life, I have felt obligated to give a reason if I ever said no to someone. And if I couldn't think of a reason, I would say yes, even when I really wanted or needed to say no. I think I felt like if I didn't have a good enough reason, then saying no would be selfish or mean. I was also afraid others would get angry or hurt which might lead them to reject or abandon me. I ended up doing a lot of things out of obligation and found myself in situations I didn't want to be in.

One problem with excuses is that whenever I begin to explain why I am saying no, I am automatically asking, *Is this a good enough reason? And will they think this is a good enough reason?* I am inviting the other person to judge my reasoning and therefore create an opportunity for them to oppose my excuse or to offer solutions that will enable me (in theory) to turn that 'no' into a 'yes'; and if that happens, where does that leave me? Pretty much back where I started. I either have to say yes now that I am all out of excuses, or I can reiterate my 'no,' this time realizing I'm better off just saying no—excuse free. A simple 'no' eliminates the dynamic of inviting others to evaluate or judge my decisions and my priorities. A simple 'no' says "This is me, and this is what I need," rather than "Is my decision OK with you? Will you still approve of me? (Please say yes!)"

Considering and giving my own heart priority also leads me to simple honesty within myself as I make decisions. Not only am I not required to give my reason for saying no, I am not even required to *have* a good reason. If my heart is saying no, then let me just say no—even when I don't completely understand why. It is OK to say no just because my heart is saying no.

Where does it come from, this notion that we 'should' or 'ought' to do this or that? 'Should' and 'ought' are words that generally preface what we believe to be the 'right' thing to do. We mistakenly equate saying yes with 'rightness.' Saying yes is not always right. In fact, saying yes may actually be the wrong thing because we are saying it much too often, and for all the wrong reasons. We say yes because we think we 'should,' yet our 'yes' and the actions that follow are not coming from the heart. In this, we perpetuate an unhealthy dynamic within our relationships wherein we are continually building secret resentments, failing to draw healthy boundaries, and disrespecting our own hearts and the hearts of others. We do a great disservice to ourselves and to others when we base our decisions on 'shoulds' and 'oughts.'

Of course, there is a place for doing something we don't feel like doing. There is a place for self-denial and making a decision to serve another out of love, but let it come from the heart. Let it not be a 'should' that is feeding any undealt with need to please, an avoidance of disapproval, or a lack of healthy boundaries. If I am doing it because I feel guilt that I 'should' do it, then I would much better love and serve my own heart and the other person to say 'no,' and afterwards, to examine the emotions that arise out of that decision.

STREAMS OF LIVING WATER

Living from the heart, we begin to operate in a new way in all of these areas both naturally—in a way that flows out of us without even trying—as well as by choice.

In the process of healing, we are daily being restored and re-wired. We will often find that our inclinations have shifted toward these new ways of thinking, relating, and living—toward vulnerability, trust, respect, responsibility, healthy boundaries, and simple honesty. Throughout my healing journey, I have often noticed myself responding to a situation differently than how I once would have, or letting go of something very easily that I would have struggled with before.

Yet we must still choose. We are continually being presented with situations that require us to make decisions—now with a new understanding of what compelled us to what we chose before, and a knowing of what our hearts need for us to choose this time around. We are learning, growing, and understanding more every day as we walk through this process; and because we are becoming healed and therefore wholehearted, we are able to choose now what considers and honors our own hearts, and to make decisions that demonstrate true love and respect for the hearts of others.

QUESTIONS TO CONSIDER

Can you identify any ways that you tend to practice self-protection rather than vulnerability? Are there any fears that come up at the thought of being vulnerable? Can you put words to the fears?

Are there any areas of your life in which you are aware of having a need to feel 'in control?' What is the fear attached to not having control?

Do you find yourself dwelling on the past? Do you find yourself waiting for any future pictures to materialize? Considering your answers, are either of these preventing you from living in, and truly enjoying, your present?

You are The Brave One, the unafraid one

Who looks suffering in the eye and does not run

Our true names arise when the time comes

And you are The Brave One

ANDY GULLAHORN

"THE BRAVE ONE" FROM THE ALBUM
EVERYTHING AS IT SHOULD BE

CHAPTER 16

Getting My Life Back

DURING MY SEASON OF HEALING, I EXPERIENCED A SERIES of dreams, which I believe were from the Lord. The dreams happened over the course of about two years, and always in the dreams, the Lord was highlighting to me a man that I knew. As a thirty-something single with a desire for marriage and motherhood, I often assumed God was highlighting this man to me through dreams because I was meant to marry him. Yet in person, we seemed to be like oil and water—we didn't mix. Something about me pushed his buttons and any move I made toward him was almost always met with awkwardness or contempt or what I perceived as rejection. After two years of wrestling with the Lord over the dreams and not being able to find resolve or relief, I sat with my counselor one day, and through my tears, voiced my weariness and my frustration with this man with whom I could find no peace or common ground, with the situation, and with God.

For the longest time, I had felt committed to seeing things through because of the dreams—because I truly believed that the dreams were from God. I was learning to let go of needing to know the outcome;

that rather than being invested in an outcome, my job was to be invested in His goodness. To trust that He was doing something good, no matter what. I was learning about deep trust—not trusting Him to give me the outcome I was hoping for—just *trusting Him.*

But on this day, sitting in front of my counselor, I had come to the place of wanting to walk away from it all. It had become an intensely painful situation. Because it was being played out parallel to my healing journey, I had purposely been working to stay soft-hearted, to love without agenda, and trying *not* to self-protect, judge, or control. I was being set-up constantly. And from this man, I was mostly feeling contempt, rejection, walls, and judgment. I felt vulnerable and I didn't want to do it anymore. An old familiar feeling came knocking...*tap, tap, tap.* It had always been my "go-to." *Write him off.* It always makes me feel safe—writing someone off always gives me the upper hand. Walking away requires no risk and no trust. *Forget this—it's not worth it.* Move on to the next thing, the next adventure, the next person.

My counselor had known of the dreams, had known the person and the situation. After sitting with me and listening to my heart on this day, knowing I was ready to throw in the towel, she said something to me that I will never forget. She said, "Chalis, you can choose to walk away from this. But if you do, down the road you will find yourself in the same situation with someone else, and it will continue to happen. **To get Life from this, you must go into the pain and see it all the way through to the other side. If you do, then you will come out the other side** *with your Life.*"

I knew she was right. Through her words, the Lord was offering me Life. This was an invitation. Will you trust Me? Will you walk a little while longer with Me through this?

Shortly after this, I received my breakthrough in what turned out to be one of the most poignant and transcendent moments of my life. I have never experienced anything like it before or since.

A situation arose involving this man that at first felt like an arrow of contempt had been aimed straight for my heart and released. My knee-jerk reaction was to be mortified and angry. Yet now that I was operating with a deeper awareness of my own heart and my emotions, I was surprised to discover in the moments that followed this initial blow, that I wasn't really feeling the way I thought I would feel. Instead, as I continued to process the situation, I felt myself being infused with something so solid, so true, so pure, like liquid gold. It was the reality of who I am, becoming real to me. It was memories of hundreds of little darts of contempt, disregard, disrespect, or rejection from this man, all becoming null and void, evaporating like a mist. It was scales falling off of my eyes and for the first time, seeing *and believing* my true value, my true worth in this moment. The healing, the change had already taken place within me, but this was my moment of recognition—when all that God had changed and healed in me was being revealed to me through the test of this fiery arrow of contempt. It was bringing into razor-sharp focus this truth for me: *that no one in this whole wide world can change who I am or define me in any way.*

I felt like Neo, marveling at the bullets that were approaching him in slow motion, rendered powerless because of His true identity. (He's The One!) In the final scene from The Matrix, Neo is simultaneously gaining the revelation of who he is and discovering with wonder what that means in this particularly dire situation. It means he is able to deflect scores of bullets and defeat an army of armed robots with nary an effort. *Brilliant.*

The moral of the story is: I made a decision to go into the pain. Rather than walking away or writing someone off, I chose to believe that God was working on my behalf. I didn't know what He was doing, what His purpose was for drawing this situation out, but I kept walking with Him through it. By this I mean that I continued to pray and believe God would show me...something. I didn't know what it was, but I knew He wanted to do something. Because I did not feel released to forget it and move on, I just stayed 'in it.' I kept my heart soft, and yes, vulnerable.

I went into the pain, and I saw it through all the way to the other side. I found my Life on the other side, because through it, I was given the gift of the revelation of who I am. I learned that I am strong, that I am beautiful just as I am, I am delightful, and I am loved.

WITH MY WHOLE BEING

The journey toward living authentically involves acknowledging the importance of *every* aspect of our being. Our emotions are just as much an important part of who we are as our mind and will, our body, and our spirit. We are designed to experience life with all of the aspects of who we are connected and healthy, not fragmented and broken, but whole. This allows us to live conscious of our hearts, and for our hearts to be fully awake, present, and engaged. It was never intended that we compartmentalize (even vilify) certain parts of ourselves, especially in the way that many of us have learned to lock some parts away, never acknowledging or addressing them at all. I am talking about unprocessed grief, hurts, anger, desire, needs, hopes, and unexplored gifts.

Don't forget to laugh, and don't be afraid to cry. Laughter and tears are two of the greatest gifts of the human experience. Laughter, that 'good medicine,' brings relief, release, and pleasure, even in the midst of our struggles, pain, and questions; and our tears are connected to both inexpressible joy and deepest sorrow, profound human empathy, and glimpses of overwhelming and utterly transcendent truth, beauty, and love.

Consequently, when we have lost our ability to laugh and to cry, we have lost something that is vital to authentic living. Two essential ingredients have been left out of the recipe, and without them, life doesn't taste quite like the real thing.

QUESTIONS TO CONSIDER

Considering your current daily life, can you think of a situation that has triggered within you feelings of wanting to shut down, walk away, or 'throw in the towel?'

Crying is a natural physical response to a vast spectrum of emotions, including sadness, grief, joy, and even feeling loved. How do you handle it when the tears want to come? Do you allow yourself to cry, or do you try to hold back your tears? However you answered, write about why.

Consider the physical, emotional, mental, and spiritual aspects of yourself. Are there one or more aspects that you have spent time developing to the neglect of the others? If so, is there a neglected aspect of yourself that you would like to begin to focus on? Write about your answer.

Restoration

I TALKED BRIEFLY ABOUT THE GREAT LOSS IN CHAPTER ONE, and how it affects each of us differently, whether it comes during childhood, as a teenager, or through losses, betrayals, or painful circumstances of adulthood. Because we live in a broken world, we cannot escape the fact that none of us will experience life perfectly, as it was meant to be experienced and lived. We have all to some degree lost our 'best life,' at least in the fullest, most complete sense of what could have been.

The Great Loss touches all of us in some way. Yet we are not left without the hope of restoration and redemption. Jesus gave His life, dying and then overcoming death to live again so that we, too, could experience resurrection life, being brought by His healing power to live as we were created to live—authentically, in fullness of joy, freedom and love.

So if the ability to experience and express our true emotions has been lost, let it be restored. If the voice of our heart has been silenced because of false beliefs perpetuated through the generations, let it be restored. If by killing or burying our longings, we find that we are numb, asleep, or simply existing, let us be awakened.

And if tragically, we have lost who we are amidst the systems we have employed to survive and the masks we have grown accustomed to wearing, then let us resolve to take a journey; setting out to find the buried treasure that is our very own pure and true heart. Let us adventure with the help of the Holy Spirit to rescue and return that precious treasure, and experience the sweet, promised restoration and redemption of all that has been lost.

And when restoration has taken place, when the beauty of experiencing and expressing the depths of our true emotions is returned to us, and when we have been awakened from our slumber and the voice of our heart is restored, let us find ourselves re-centered and settling into the very middle of our own authentic life—really living and experiencing our life as it was meant to be.

May Light always surround you;
Hope kindle and rebound you.
May your Hurts turn to Healing;
Your Heart embrace Feeling.
May Wounds become Wisdom;
Every Kindness a Prism.
May Laughter infect you;
Your Passion resurrect you.
May Goodness inspire
your Deepest Desires.
Through all that you Reach For,
May your arms Never Tire.

D. SIMONE

ACKNOWLEDGEMENTS

DEEPEST GRATITUDE GOES TO MY HUSBAND, SHANE, who has championed the writing of this book more tirelessly than I could have ever hoped was reasonable, and to my treasures, Yona and Ezra, who keep me returning daily to the beautiful Present; to our extended family—who love us and still give us space to see things differently; a big thank you to Kara, Jenna, Emelie, Christine, Dave, Rowena, Lacee and Nicole—your courageous and invaluable input and your encouragement have challenged me to dig up the best possible version of this book; to Andi Cumbo-Floyd, whose wise advice gave me courage to step into a deeper, more personal telling of my own story; to Shane Kingery, good friend and stellar designer—so thankful for your creativity, your stunning work, and your enthusiasm for this project; to Pat Stark, my counselor, mentor, and friend who has shared these principles with me and walked me through the healing process—thank you. Above all, I thank God for healing me, for the grace and the words to express it in writing, and for surrounding me with people who would help bring this book to life.

Thanks be to God Who gives us the victory through our Lord, Jesus Christ. 1 Corinthians 15:57

APPENDIX A: SURVIVAL SYSTEMS
(Compiled by Pat Stark)

Survival Systems are all of the different ways we wear a mask. When as a child, being myself gets me hurt or rejected, I figure out how to become more 'acceptable.' These are all of the ways we learned to keep ourselves safe, to gain approval, to earn acceptance, to be loved. This is what we did to survive.

On Survival Systems Pat writes:
Survival Systems are our hiding places—we use them to hide our true selves and to try to escape our buried pain. They are self-protective strategies we have devised that keep our hearts covered and ourselves feeling safe. They are a false self, our 'fig leaves.' They are masks we wear to cover our true selves, idols we trust in instead of having to trust God, false images we have to continually keep propped up—illusions.

Survival Systems are fueled by the false belief that we are a failure or not enough in our true selves. They ease our pain and cover our shame lies. They feel like 'us' but are just what covers us. Our false self is what God is shaking us free from, but it feels like we are being destroyed. But we are not—just the covering system we learned to operate in since experiencing the hurts of childhood.

"For we have made a lie our refuge and falsehood our hiding place." (Isaiah 28:15 NIV)

Our only true hiding place: **"For you died, and your life is now hidden with Christ in God." (Colossians 3:3 NIV)**

Addictions, Compulsions, or Escape Places: alcohol, drugs, movies, TV, Internet, porn, sex, computer games, Facebook or social media, gambling, people, food, sweets, work, pleasure; even Bible or prayer can be used to escape pain and the realities of life in a broken world.

All-or-Nothing Thinking

Anger—Arrogance

Argumentativeness

Avoidance or **Blame** of Self or Others

Beating Yourself Up with words

Being Nice (Kind is a Bible word, not Nice)

Body Image

Busyness

Care-taking of Others

Collecting People—need for popularity, people addiction

Contempt of Self or Others—even through sarcasm or humor, lack of respect

Control (Domination, Manipulation, Intimidation) —Self, Others, Key People, Circumstances, God (through prayer or being 'good')

Dreamer

Excusing instead of facing truth and taking responsibility

Failure—not trying, sabotaging success

False Beauty (image)

False Order that is really just Control—need to have all your ducks lined up in a row

False Peacemaker—peace at any cost

False Positivism instead of living in true reality that has "mixture"

False Spiritualism that further feeds the separation of our soul and spirit (instead of uniting them)

False Strength or Learned Helplessness so others will take care of you

Fantasy

Getting Ahead of where you currently are in thinking about situations—drawing conclusions

Hiding Self

Hoarding

Holding Self Back in relationships and only speaking what others want to hear

Intellect

Judgments/Criticism

Lack of Self-Care—body, soul, or spirit

Measured Words, Over-thinking

Negativism "If I expect the worst, I won't feel disappointed"

Over-Attention to One Part of life to the exclusion of others Example: Talents, Career, Exercise

Over-attention to Outward Appearances of Self, Work, Things, Others, Home, Car, Materialism, Money, Creating an Image or Illusion

Over-collecting things

Over-efficiency

People-Pleasing

Performance to cover Shame

Perfectionism

Procrastination

Rebelliousness

Religious Spirit

Selling Soul to keep your own world feeling safe

Sports

Success—trying too hard

Superior Attitude, Pride, or Shaming Others

TV, Movies, Books

Using Various Roles to Hide in (Example: motherhood, boss, ministering)

Wanting to be Noticed (especially by authority figures)

Work or Career

APPENDIX B: LIST OF NEGATIVE EMOTIONS
(Written and Compiled by Pat Stark)

Below is a list of words that can help us identify specific negative emotions we are experiencing. Being specific is important because it allows us to connect the present emotion with a specific situation or hurt from the past. This allows us to grieve our true losses and find healing for our hearts.

ANGER

Aggression

Annoyed

Antagonizing

Argumentative

Arrogant

Bitterness

Combative

Contemptuous

Depression

   (Anger turned in at Self)

Disrespectful

Envious

Flaring Temper

Frustrated

Full of Rage

Furious

Haughty Independence

Hostile

Irritated

Misundaerstood

Outraged

Overwhelmed

Powerless

Punishing

Rebellious

Resentful

Revengeful

Slow Boil

Sulky

Tantrums

Unappreciated

Violated

Walked on/Mistreated/
   Betrayed

Wrathful

FEAR

Agitated

Alarmed

Alone

Anguished

Anxious

Apprehensive

Controlling

Cornered

Cursed

Cut Off

Desolate

Disquieted

Fear of being Abandoned

Fear of being Discovered

Fear of being Exposed

Fear of being Rejected

Fear of being Shamed

Fear of being Thrown Away

Fear of Weakness

Fearing or using Control

Forsaken

Helpless

Hopeless

Insecure

Out of Control

Over-concerned

Overwhelmed

Panicked

Powerless

Scared

Terrified

Troubled

Unbelieving

Uneasy

Unlovable

Unprotected

Unsupported

Vulnerable

Worried

GUILT: REAL OR FALSE GUILT

All My Fault

Always Wrong

Always feeling Guilty

Blamed/Blamer

Can't Do Anything Right

Compartmentalized

Condemned

Critical

Defeated

Defenseless

Despair

Disconnected

Disgraceful or Dirty

Hiding Self

GUILT: REAL OR FALSE GUILT
(continued)

Invisible

Isolated

Jealous

Judged

Judgmental

Learned Helplessness

Overwhelmed

Paralyzed

Powerless

Pressure to Perform

Self-condemning

Self-disgust

Self-hate

Self-punishing

Self-sabotaging

Shameful

Undesirable

Unlovable

Useless

HURT

Abandoned

Abused

Accused

Annihilated

Avoided

Betrayed

Cheated

Crushed

Cut Off

Deceived

Defrauded

Deprived

Deserted

Devalued

Disappointed

Discouraged

Disregarded

Disrespected

Excluded

Feeling Useless

Forsaken

Frightened

Grieved

Heartbroken

Ignored

Injured

Insensitive to My Needs

Left Out

Lied To

Lonely

Misunderstood

Neglected

HURT

(continued)

Not Cared For

Not Belonging

Not Valued

Offended

Put Down

Rejected

Ridiculed

Sad

Shattered

Suspicious

Unfairly Judged

Unimportant

Unnoticed

Used

Walked On

Wounded

SHAME: REAL OR FALSE

(Buried Shame can come out as Pride)

Abusive or Abused

Embarrassed

Exploited

Fear of Humiliation

Feeling like a Failure

Forgotten

Forsaken

Hopeless

Impure

Inadequate

Incompetent

Inferior

Insecure

Insignificant

Isolated

Lost

Needing to Be Seen

No Good

Not Belonging

Not Cared For

Not Chosen

Not Measuring Up

Not Needed

Not Valued

Self-disgust

Self-hatred

Self-sabotaging

Unheard or Unseen

Unimportant

Unwanted

Unworthy

Useless

Valueless

Wanting to Hide

Weak

Worthless

BOOKS

Boundaries by Henry Cloud and John Townsend

Bold Love by Dan Allender

Born to Fly by Pat Stark

Cry of the Soul by Dan Allender

Daring Greatly by Brene Brown

Facing Codependency by Pia Melody

God is Good by Bill Johnson

Hinds' Feet on High Places by Hannah Hurnard

Jesus Said to Her by Skip Moen

Keep Your Love On by Danny Silk

Lifting the Mask by Jo Naughton

Lost Heart? by Pat Stark and Nicole Welch

Search for Significance by Robert McGee

Shame: Identity Thief by Henry Malone and John Sanford

Spiritual Slavery to Spiritual Sonship by Jack Frost

The Artist's Way by Julia Cameron

The Choice by Dr. Edith Eva Eger

The Journey of Desire by John Eldridge

The Story of Life by Pat Stark

Wild at Heart by John Eldredge

Wounded Heart by Dan Allender

ONLINE RESOURCES

AdamYoungCounseling.com

BethelSozo.com

ElijahHouse.org | *"Bitter Roots Judgment" and "Heart of Stone/ Inner Vows" free audio teaching*

GetHeartMedia.com

JoNaughton.com

LoveDweller.com

LovingOnPurpose.com

PatrickDoyle.life

RansomedHeart.com

TheAllenderCenter.org

TheCovenantCenter.com

VeritasCounseling.com

ABOUT THE AUTHOR

CHALIS BUTLER WRITES FROM HER FAVORITE OVERSTUFFED chair in sunny, Central Florida. In the throws of parenting two toddlers, she and her husband vacillate between intentional living and survival mode. This is why her house can look immaculate or appalling on any given day. She has a rocky relationship with coffee. She wears graphic T's and yoga shorts whenever possible. She loves finding awesome books for a dollar, watching her kids sleep, and pie crust.

Some other interesting tidbits: Chalis has spent time working with mission teams and teaching English in Haiti; she lived and worked in Australia for three years before returning home to the United States; she spent 16 years teaching music before switching gears to become a stay-at home mom and begin working on her first book. You can find her online at LoveDweller.com.